THE NEW AND COMPLETE GUIDE TO DAY TRADING

2021 EDITION

Contents

- Introduction 6
- HISTORY OF DAY TRADING 8
  - **How Day Trading Decisions Are Made** 19
  - **How Day Trading Works** 20
  - The Basics of Day Trading 23
  - Setting Realistic Profit Targets in Trading 25
  - Day by day Goals 26
  - Week by week and Monthly Goals 28
  - Advantages of Day Trading 35
  - Day Trading Risks 36
  - **Chapter 3 Psychology and Mindset** 42
    - **Do Not Rationalize Your Trading Errors** 42
    - **Beware of Your Trading Decisions** 44
    - **Keep Your Emotions in Check** 46
    - **Be Patient When Trading** 48
- WHAT ARE THE RIGHT REQUIREMENTS FOR DAY TRADING 50
- CONTROLLED RISK AND RETURN RATIO IN DAY TRADING 56
  - Case of the Risk/Reward Ratio being used 59
  - Chapter 4 Tools of the Trade 61
    - **The Broker** 61
    - **Minimum Equity Requirement** 62
    - **Direct-Access and Conventional Brokers** 64

- **The Trading Platform** 65
- **Real Time Market Data** 66
- **The Day Trading Orders** 67
- **Hardware** 68
- **Stock Pick Scanners and Watchlists** 69
- **Day Trading Community** 70
- **Get Your Education** 71
- **Build Your Business Plan** 72
- **Make Sure You Have the Right Supplies** 72
- **Have Enough Cash** 73

THE BEST STRATEGIES AND TECHNIQUES TO START WITH DAY TRADING 74

STRATEGIES 75

Trading Strategies for Beginners 77

5 Day Trading Strategies 80

    3. Momentum 82

Risk Management 88

    Stop-misfortune 88

    Position size 88

DAY TRADING TECHNIQUES 91

TECHNICAL ANALYSIS OF DAY TRADING 92

Value, Volume, and Volatility Run in Distinct Trends 96

Types of Charts 99

Money Management 127

Choose The Right Lot Size Based On Your Capital 128

Using Standard Lots 129

Learn, Learn and Learn 129

Use only a reputable broker 130

Utilize a practice account 131

Keep Your Charts clean 131

Stop Loss Order Is Not Just For Preventing Losses 132

THE BEST INDICATORS FOR INEXPERIENCED TRADERS 133

1) Bollinger Bands 137

2) Ichimoku Kinko Hyo (AKA Ichimoku Cloud) 140

3) Relative Strength Index (RSI) 144

4) Moving Average Convergence Divergence (MACD) 147

5) Parabolic Stop and Reverse (SAR) 151

6) Stochastic 152

7) Average Directional Index (ADX) 155

RSI and Bollinger Bands 159

WHAT STRATEGIES DO NOT FOLLOW IF YOU ARE EXPERT TRADER 163

Avoid strategies with a massively enormous stop misfortune 170

Building up Your Watch List 173

Decide Which of These Stocks Work Best for You 173

Put That Entry and Exit Strategy in Place 174

Purchase the Stocks You Want 175

Pay Attention to the Market Until the Trade Is Closed 175

Take Some Time to Reflect on That Trade and Write Down Some of the Information as Research Later 176

Choosing and Purchasing Stocks 177

Knowing How to Stop Loss 178

Knowing When to Sell 180

Conclusion 182

Introduction

Day trading entails buying and selling of stocks within the same day. It enables you grow your income through making profit from stock price changes that occur during the day. To successfully engage in day trading, it is important to understand how it works.

Apart from knowledge associated with basic trading, day traders must also keep track of the latest stock market news and analysis that can affect or impact their stocks. They must be aware of breaking news and the economic outlook held by experts.

Day trading requires a trader to put in at least four to five hours every day. It will be best not to take it up if you are unable to dedicate at least this much time. It takes time and effort to spot trends and capitalize on them. It will be important to move fast and make quick moves to make the most of the investment opportunities.

When you are just starting as a day trader, it will be best to focus on just one or two stocks and track their movement. It is easier to track limited stocks instead of focusing on too many. Smaller amounts invested in stocks will make it easier to track them and assess how your investment is doing. Buying fractions of a stock is a good idea for beginners.

It is always best to remain calm and collected, especially when the market is moving unpredictably. This is a characteristic that all day traders must possess to make the most of their trades. Your stock decisions should be based on logic and not impulsiveness.

You must always have a plan of action ready. Successful traders will be able to move fast between plans and maintain decorum while trading. It will be best to stick with a winning formula compared to chasing profits. Most traders follow a set philosophy that states it is important to plan your trades instead of allowing emotions to guide you.

This book explains it all and provides the reader with the steps he needs to know in order to become a successful day trader, the book does not promise the reader to turn into a rich man in few days but it guarantees to put the reader on the correct road become one in a very short term.

This book will teach committed readers the basics of Day trading that they can practice as soon as they are done reading it, it is explained, in simple and not complex terms and it will allow beginners to start day trading immediately and intermediate traders to triple their profits and minimize their losses. So, lets start!

HISTORY OF DAY TRADING

In the past, the main individuals who had the option to exchange effectively in the securities exchange were those working for enormous money related establishments, businesses, and trading houses. With the ascent of the web and web-based trading houses, specialists have made it simpler for the average individual investor to get in on the game.

Day trading can end up being an extremely rewarding vocation, as long as you do it appropriately. It can likewise be a touch of trying for fledglings—particularly for the individuals who aren't completely arranged with an allaround arranged strategy. Indeed, even the most prepared day traders can hit unpleasant fixes and experience misfortunes. What precisely is day trading, and how can it work?

In present-day times, we underestimate day trading. It sounds good to us that somebody can purchase a stock and sell it around the same time.

Be that as it may, day trading is a moderately new idea. The history of day trading has experienced numerous exciting bends in the road throughout the years, yet it has never been more conspicuous than it is today.

When did the day trading start? To what extent has day trading existed? You are going to know it all you have to think about the history of day trading.

1867: The Day Trading Starts with the Ticker Tape

Day trading can be followed right back to 1867. In spite of what numerous individuals accept, day trading didn't rise with the ascent of PCs or the web. Truth be told, it follows its history back to even before power.

Day trading can be followed back to 1867. Not long after the broadcast was concocted, financial exchanges utilized the transits' correspondence innovation to make the primary ticker tape. Ticker tape made it simple to impart data about exchanges happening on the trading floor with representatives.

Before the web and other worldwide correspondence stages were created, intermediaries would attempt to live in closeness to trades like the New York Stock Exchange, as it implied they were getting a consistent stockpile of ticker tape with the most modern data.

Today, ticker tape alludes to the flood of electronic data spilling over a standard. In days passed by, it was a physical piece of paper. Merchants would utilize ticker tape to settle on educated choices on securities exchange developments for the duration of the day, taking into account a few intermediaries to take an interest in day trading.

All through the early history of securities exchanges, singular traders didn't have direct access to markets. All requests were put through a merchant. Merchants utilized data gathered off the ticker tape.

This type of trading was normal all through the beginning of securities exchanges. Be that as it may, the obstructions to section implied day trading was not well known among the all-inclusive community.

1971: A Communication Network is made

In 1971, the spread of financial exchange data around the globe turned out to be more effective than any time in recent memory. That year, the (NASD) made an electronic correspondence organize (ECN). That ECN was known as the National Association of Securities Dealers Automated Quotation System. Today, we know it as the NASDAQ.

An ECN is characterized as any PC framework that encourages money related items exchanges outside of stock trades. This assisted with opening financial exchanges and investing in singular investors – not simply specialists.

Out of nowhere, a wide range of trading – including day trading – were increasingly open to the average man. Be that as it may, it was as yet far away from turning into a famous or normal action among smalltime, singular investors.

1975: Fixed Commission Exchanges Are Abolished

For the whole early history of American financial exchanges (180 years), there were fixed rates on exchanges. Markets had fixed costs on all exchanges, which implied that representatives couldn't contend with different agents on cost.

That changed in 1975 and changed the financial exchange world until the end of time.

That implied, without precedent for a long time, trading expenses on securities exchanges were chosen by market rivalry – which appears as though a fitting method to choose things identified with the financial exchange.

In light of these changes, Charles Schwab and different firms started permitting clients to exchange stocks at limited commission rates, denoting the start of the rebate specialist period. Intermediaries started to contend with each other by offering lower and lower rates. These merchants began to develop and explore different avenues regarding new trading frameworks that made the procedure progressively effective.

By and by, trading stocks turned out to be a lot simpler for singular investors. Not exclusively would they be able to completely get to securities exchanges, yet they could do it at a lower cost from a developing number of agents, a large number of which emerged during this timeframe to address requests.

The ECNs Make Trading Easier for the Average Investor

Various Electronic Communication Networks (ECNs) would show up over the coming years, including notable names like Instinet (which despite everything exists right up 'til today, and was really established before NASDAQ, in 1969).

These ECNs emerged to address the interest of investors. Driven by another time of serious commission rates, ECNs had the option to serve a developing scope of customers. ECNs had an essential job in the market: they were mechanized frameworks that coordinated the purchase and sale orders for protections.

All the more critically, ECNs associated singular traders with significant financiers, permitting either side to purchase/sell protections from the other without experiencing a go-between. This drove costs down much further, making day trading significantly simpler.

During this period, ECNs like Instinet, SelectNet, and NYSE Arca would all get conspicuous in the business.

Instinet is the most popular and was broadly utilized all through the 1970s, 80s, and 90s for NASDAQ exchanges. Some portion of its prevalence was that people and little firms could likewise utilize it.

SelectNet, then again, was utilized fundamentally by market creators. Right up 'til today, it doesn't require prompt request execution. It's utilized to assist investors with trading with explicit market producers.

NYSE Arca was an ECN that rise out of a mix of the NYSE and Archipelago, an early ECN from 1996. It encourages electronic stock trading on significant US trades – like the NYSE and NASDAQ.

By 1999, day trading had become an all-out wonder.

Be that as it may, in contrast with day trading today, there weren't the same number of day traders as you're likely reasoning. It was something or other that many individuals heard individuals did – however few "average" individuals really took an interest in.

As a demonstration of that reality, Arthur Levitt, Chairman of the SEC, affirmed before Congress in 1999 and assessed that the number of day traders was around 7,000.

In correlation, Mr. Levitt assessed that there were roughly 5 million web clients bought into online merchants.

In the same way as other things individuals didn't comprehend, day trading became dreaded and questioned. During this timeframe, day trading had a negative meaning. The pessimistic disposition towards day trading finished in a shooting binge at an Atlanta day trading office, where Mark Barton killed 12 individuals and harmed 13 increasingly subsequent to losing an expected $105,000 in day trading over a multi-month time span.

The Barton episode persuaded numerous individuals that day trading was so unpleasant it could persuade an in any case common man to submit mass homicide.

Day trading as a calling endured another shot when, two weeks after the Barton shootings, the North American Securities Administrators Association discharged a report expressing that 7 out of 10-day traders lose everything. They don't simply lose money generally – they lose all that they've contributed.

2000: The SOES was changed to take out the advantages for day traders, yet the greatest blow came as another financial exchange breakdown. At the point when the website bubble burst, a significant number of the daytrading go-getters, either bankrupted or terrified away, looked for new vocations.

2008: The rebellious, boondocks sentiment of day trading is a distant memory, as are the majority of the make easy money hopefuls. In its place are proficient day traders who seek after their work with a similar industriousness and care as some other expert.

What is Day Trading?

Day trading is the buying and selling of securities in one single trading day. This can occur in any type of marketplace that you choose but it is most common in the stock market and in the forex market.

Day trading is very fast paced. You will purchase a stock, bond, option or other security at some point during the day. Then, sometime during the same day, you will sell the security. If you watched the market properly and the trade goes well, you will make a profit from that sale. If you made a mistake with your calculations, you will lose money.

Day trading is a strategy of trading financial securities, such as stocks and currencies, where positions are taken and closed within the same day. Also called short trading, it involves buying a financial security and selling them before the trading day closes.

How short can day trading last? It can be as short as buying and selling in a few minutes, or even seconds! The point is to end the trading day with a square position, i.e., neither long nor short on any financial security.

It doesn't matter how many trades you do during the day. You can trade just once a day or 10 times a day...it doesn't matter. The defining characteristic of day trading is ending the day with a square position.

Day trading can take place in any market, but the most common ones are the stock market and foreign exchange or forex markets.

When you start day trading, you'll need to start looking at financial securities from a different vantage point. For example, if you're used to swing trading or a buy-and-hold approach to stock market investing, you'll need to look at stocks differently when you day trade if you want to profit from it.

Instead of having a longer-term perspective on stocks, you'll need to reorient it to a very short-term one. In particular, you should shift your focus from a company's possible growth over the long term to its possible immediate price actions during the day.

Another area where you'll need to reorient your thinking are gains. Instead of looking at substantial gains, e.g., 10% or more, you'll need to scale down. Given the short time frame, you may have to make do with gains as low as 1% to 2%. This is because day trading involves trading at a higher frequency but with smaller gains, which accumulate over time.

You do not want to let your trade go on to the next day. This requires a different type of strategy than you will use with day trading. Mixing strategies during the same trade just to avoid a loss will actually make things worse. It is better to cut your losses with that trade and move on, closing out the trade before the end of the day.

With day trading, you are not going to make a ton of money off each trade. In fact, if you make a few dollars with each trade, you are doing a good job. The point here is to do a lot of little trades, taking advantage of the temporary ups and downs of the market. A lot of little profits can add up to a good payday when the process is done.

The potential profit that you can make from day traded is often misunderstood on Wall Street. There are many internet scams that like to take on this confusion and capitalize on it making a ton of money by promising large returns in a short period of time. On the other side, the media continues to promote this trading method as a get rich quick scheme.

To determine whether you will be successful depends on a few important factors. Mainly, if you jump into the day trading game without enough knowledge about the market and how this trading method works, you will probably fail. But there are many day traders who are able to make a successful living from day trading. These individuals know about the market, have a good strategy in place, and can work with the market, despite the risks.

Day trading can be difficult. There are many professional financial advisors and money managers who worry about the risk of day trading and will shy away from it. They worry that in many cases, the reward is not going to justify all the risk that you take with day trading. It is possible to make a profit in this method but you have to really know the market and you must have the time to fully watch the market at all times while completing your trade. Even those who do well in day trading will admit that the success rate with this method is often lower than the other methods of stock market trading.

Day trading isn't just restricted to stocks. You can day trade currencies, you can day trade commodities as well as options. Day trading involves more of a set of practices that you stick to.

Day trading is the very definition of short term trading. It's all about the short term. In fact, your trading horizon is restricted to one day. This means that you open a position and you close it strictly within one day's trading hours. You engage in it daily, you focus on one or more stocks or one or more commodities or currency pairings or options.

It's important to keep in mind that all your positions are liquidated by the end of the day. Whether you make money or not, you are out of your position by the end of the day. That is the key definition of day trading.

How Day Trading Decisions Are Made

A day trader's decision whether to enter a stock or exit a stock all boils down to the probable movement of the pricing of the stock within the trading period. The trading period can be as short as 5 minutes or less or it can be the whole day. Whatever the case may be, it doesn't exceed the whole day.

Day traders make money off volatility. They do not make as much money when the stock is trading sideways for a long time and gradually slopes up. A stock might gain value 10% over the course of a year, but that stock, for all intents and purposes, is off limits to a day trader because the volatility isn't there. They would rather trade a stock that bounces 15% up and down, every single day. That stock has enough internal volatility on a day to day basis for day traders to make quite a bit of money.

What Benefit Do Day Traders Offer to the Market?

In terms of economic benefits, how does day trading benefit stock trading as a whole? Well, if anything, day traders provide liquidity to the stock market. They offer a ready base of buyers and sellers of stock. This provides the necessary movement of a stock's price that may encourage other traders to look at either the short term or long-term value and prospects of the stock. In other words, by providing action on a strictly short-term basis, day traders tend to shine a light on the overall attractiveness of a stock.

Keep in mind this is quite ironic because day traders, as a rule, do not look at the fundamentals of a stock. They don't look at the price/earnings ratio or P/E. They don't look at long term value, they don't look at industry positioning. They couldn't care less about any of that. Instead, they focus more on momentum, share movement, share volume and price velocity going either up or down.

How Day Trading Works

Once you start day trading, you can use a myriad number of techniques and methods to execute trades. For example, you can choose to trade based solely on your "gut feeling" or you can go to the other extreme of relying entirely on mathematical models that optimize trading success through elaborate automated trading systems.

Regardless of the method, you can have limitless day-trading profit potential once you master day trading. Here are some of the strategies many expert day traders use profitably.

One is what's called "trading the news", which is one of the most popular day trading strategies since time immemorial. As you may have already gleaned from the name, it involves acting upon any press-released information such as economic data, interest rates, and corporate earnings.

Another popular day trading strategy is called "fading the gap at the open". This one's applicable on trading days when a security's price opens with a gap, i.e., below the previous day's lowest price or above the previous day's highest price.

"Fading the gap at the open" means taking an opposite position from the gap's direction. If the price opens with a downward gap, i.e., below the previous day's lowest price, you buy the security. If the price opens with an upward gap, i.e., it opens higher than the previous day's highest price, you short or sell the security.

There was a time when the only people able to trade in financial markets were those working for trading houses, brokerages, and financial institutions. The rise of the internet, however, made things easier for individual traders to get in on the action. Day Trading, in particular, can be a very profitable career, as long as one goes about it in the right way.

However, it can be quite challenging for new traders, especially those who lack a good strategy. Furthermore, even the most experienced day traders hit rough patches occasionally. As stated earlier, Day Trading is the purchase and sale of an asset within a single trading day. It can happen in any marketplace, but it is more common in the stock and forex markets.

Day traders use short-term trading strategies and a high level of leverage to take advantage of small price movements in highly liquid currencies or stocks. Experienced day traders have their finger on events that lead to short-term price movements, such as the news, corporate earnings, economic statistics, and interest rates, which are subject to market psychology and market expectations.

When the market exceeds or fails to meet those expectations, it causes unexpected, significant moves that can benefit attuned day traders. However, venturing into this line of business is not a decision prospective day trader should take lightly. It is possible for day traders to make a comfortable living trading for a few hours each day.

However, for new traders, this kind of success takes time. Think like several months or more than a year. For most day traders, the first year is quite tough. It is full of numerous wins and losses, which can stretch anyone's nerves to the limit. Therefore, a day trader's first realistic goal should be to hold on to his/her trading capital.

Volatility is the name of the game when it comes to Day Trading. Traders rely on a market or stock's fluctuations to make money. They prefer stocks that bounce around several times a day, but do not care about the reason for those price fluctuations. Day traders will also go for stocks with high liquidity, which will allow them to enter and exit positions without affecting the price of the stock.

Day traders might short sell a stock if its price is decreasing or purchase if it is increasing. Actually, they might trade it several times in a day, purchasing it and short-selling it a number of times, based on the changing market sentiment. In spite of the trading strategy used, their wish is for the stock price to move.

Day Trading, however, is tricky for two main reasons. Firstly, day traders often compete with professionals, and secondly, they tend to have psychological biases that complicate the trading process.

Professional day traders understand the traps and tricks of this form of trading. In addition, they leverage personal connections, trading data subscriptions, and state-of-the-art technology to succeed. However, they still make losing trades. Some of these professionals are high-frequency traders whose aim is to skim pennies off every trade.

The Day Trading field is a crowded playground, which is why professional day traders love the participation of inexperienced traders. Essentially, it helps them make more money. In addition, retail traders tend to hold on to losing trades too long and sell winning trades too early.

Due to the urge to close a profitable trade to make some money, retail investors sort of pick the flowers and water the weeds. In other words, they have a strong aversion to making even a small loss. This tends to tie their hands behind their backs when it comes to purchasing a declining asset. This is due to the fear that it might decline further.

The Basics of Day Trading

Day trading is characterized as the buy and offer of security inside a solitary trading day. It can happen in any marketplace; however, it is generally basic in the outside trade (forex) and financial exchanges. Day traders are commonly accomplished and very much subsidized. They utilize high measures of use and transient trading strategies to gain by little value developments in exceptionally fluid stocks or monetary standards.

Day traders are receptive to occasions that cause momentary market moves. Trading the news is a well-known strategy. Planned declarations, for example, financial insights, corporate profit, or loan fees, are liable to market desires and market brain research. Markets respond when those desires are not met or are surpassed, as a rule with unexpected, noteworthy moves, which can profit day traders.

Day traders utilize various intraday strategies. These strategies include:

- Scalping, which endeavors to make various little benefits on little costs changes for the duration of the day

- Range trading, which fundamentally utilizes backing and obstruction levels to decide their purchase and sell choices

- News-based trading, which regularly holds onto trading openings from the increased volatility around news occasions

- High-recurrence trading (HFT) strategies that utilization refined calculations to misuse little or momentary market wasteful aspects

PROOF DAY TRADING

Remember that utilizing shorts, as clarified right now, not work for each trader. A few frameworks expect you to take each arrangement that goes along, regardless of whether you're up to or down, so as to exploit the edge that the framework gives.

Every trader has their own degree of hazard resistance and wanted day by day, week after week, and month to month benefit targets. Numerous fruitful traders utilize every day, week by week, month to month, and even yearly shorts.

New traders shouldn't worry about benefit objectives; however, rather, center around consistency. That being stated, what are some practical benefit objectives for a fruitful Forex trader?

Setting Realistic Profit Targets in Trading

Everything begins with defining sensible day by day objectives. Swing traders may begin with week after week objectives for evident reasons. It is imperative to set your objectives in genuine benefits, instead of pips.

It is likewise imperative to utilize a similar measure of hazard (introduction) on each exchange. Fluctuating presentation is a decent method to clear out your record – regardless of whether you're utilizing a strong trading framework.

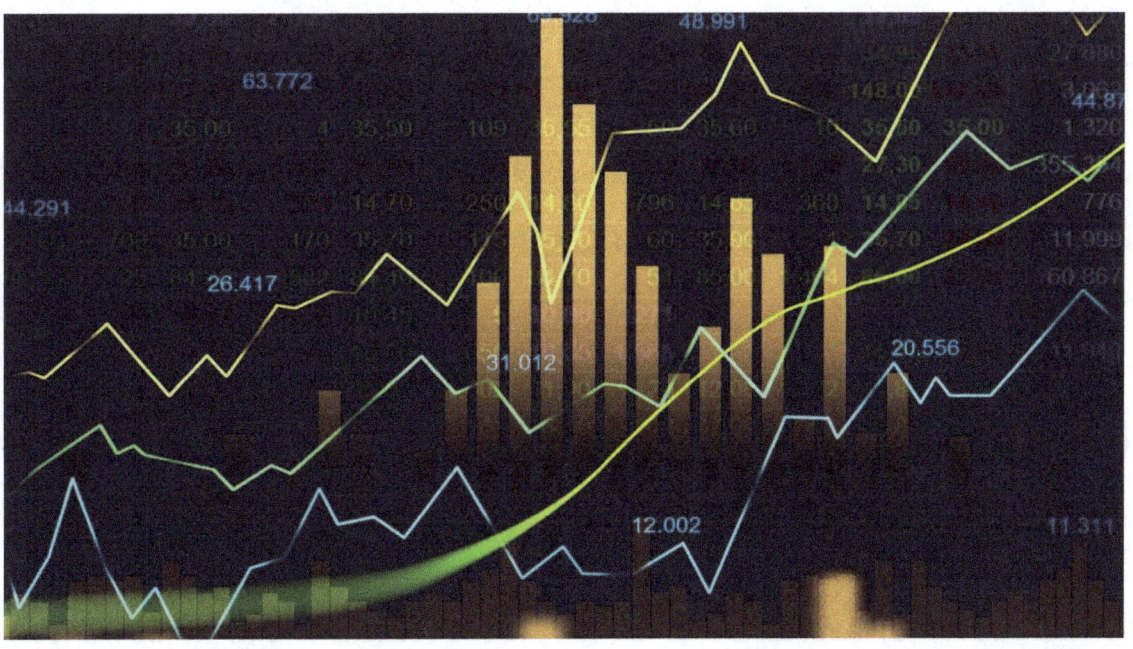

Day by day Goals

Day by day objectives is, to a great extent, controlled by your degree of hazard resistance. For example, You chance 1% per exchange. My day by day benefit cutoff is 2%, so you just need a couple of effective exchanges without any misfortunes to hit that mark.

If you are just gambling .5% per exchange, a progressively practical everyday benefit cutoff maybe 1% every day. It is going for 2%, while gambling .5%, would take two to four fruitful exchanges without any misfortunes to accomplish. At the end of the day, it's not prone to occur.

Note: Don't simply hop into the market. Gain proficiency with a decent trading framework, and afterward backtest and demo exchange until you demonstrate to yourself that you can be reliable over the long haul (months or years – not days or weeks).

At the point when you begin trading a live record, utilize the littlest part size (or the number of offers, contracts, and so forth…) accessible to you from the start. Step by step, increment your presentation per exchange to your ideal hazard level as you become acquainted with the mental obstacles of trading genuine money.

Best traders would prescribe utilizing .5 – 1% per exchange. Extremely propelled traders regularly hazard 3% or more per exchange. What amount of money would you say you will lose per exchange? When you have decided your own degree of hazard resistance, you can decide a day by day objective or cutoff.

Week by week and Monthly Goals

From that point, your week after week and month to month shorts can be set. I have a progressively forceful hazard resilience, so I may benefit cutoff targets are as per the following: 2% every day, 5% week after week, and 15% month to month. I don't utilize yearly shorts.

These objectives may appear to be high to certain traders, yet they are sensible for me.

Note: This doesn't imply that you make 2% consistently, 5% consistently, and so on…. In the event that you make 2% in a day, that is a decent day of trading. Moreover, 5% is a decent seven day stretch of trading.

If you are not reliable yet, you should concentrate on learning a beneficial trading framework and turning into a long haul, reliably productive trader. In case you're simply beginning, going for 5% every month bodes well.

If you feel that you can twofold your record at regular intervals in trading, you are not prone to set reasonable benefit targets. You will probably overtrade your way to a littler record balance.

You will chance excessively, and you will lose excessively. Ravenousness makes traders be careless and overactive in the market, which prompts botches. Little predictable and exacerbated benefits will prompt a fortune over the long haul.

Keep in mind: Money management shorts work the two different ways. In the event that you are down 2% in one day (or two misfortunes straight), Stop trading that day. Quit trading in the event that you lose 3% in a multiweek. In conclusion, Use 5% as my month to month misfortunes cutoff. Remember that you will have a progressively forceful hazard resistance.

The key advantages of turning into a day trader:

Free Information and Resources

Clearly, similar to any industry, there is a great deal of study and information to procure before plunking down before your PC and executing your first exchange. Be that as it may, an individual shouldn't be an expert in the fields of investing. There is a bounty of free assets on the Internet – and at your neighborhood library – that can help you bring your day trading profession. Obviously, you can buy day trading programming (which can run you $20-30K) that can give you moment news, outlines, and stock data, however on the off chance that you are simply starting, this could be an error.

Numerous sites offer people the chance to rehearse and learn day trading on demo programming for nothing or a little charge (nobletraders.com; thousand years traders.com).

You work for yourself.

Simply envision: you are discreetly telecommuting on your PC, executing exchanges, tasting your espresso, yet something is feeling the loss of your chief or supervisor breathing down your neck. You work for yourself. You needn't bother with demand authorization for exchanges; you don't have to fulfill another person's need; you are in the game for yourself. All things considered, you are dependable and responsible for your presentation. On the off chance that you fall flat, you lose money, conceivably an exceptionally huge sum. As much as we would all adoration this opportunity, it reminds you that you have to have the self-restraint and hardworking attitude to realize the business well.

No Overnight Risks

Probably the best favorable position of day trading is the capacity to close your situation at or before the finish of the trading day. For a day trader who opens and closes his situation before the trading day closes, the risks of holding a stock medium-term are eradicated. A conventional trader's benefits can vanish medium-term with customary, long haul trading, however, with day trading, your benefits are verified as long as you close your situations before the finish of the trading day. This permits you – on the off chance that it was a decent day – to rest adequately around evening time.

No medium-term emergencies or cataclysms in the money related markets can influence your salary for that day.

Accomplishment in Bad Market Conditions

Day traders can regularly exploit a battling market by using short-offering trading strategies to exploit falling stock costs. The capacity to bring in money off of the financial exchange in bear market conditions is a huge bit of leeway for a learned day trader.

Concentrate on Technical Analysis

There are two sorts of examination that most traders and investors look to for monetary data: technical investigation and key investigation. Customary, long haul traders have the chance to concentrate on an organization's essentials – organization wellbeing, fiscal reports, and management data – to perceive how its stock worth will change over the long haul. In spite of the fact that this is significant data to know, day traders can concentrate on technical examination for the duration of the day to make fruitful, and brisk, exchanges, bringing about benefits. This is on the grounds that a day trader is essentially worried about what is happening at the present minute, what the cost of the stock is currently, what its volume is, and what its volatility is at the present minute.

Putting many exchanges for the duration of the day, effectively observing each development of the market, and bringing in quick money are largely energizing parts of day trading. You can be in and out of exchange inside only 5 to 15 minutes. At the point when effective, seeing that you caused several dollars surprisingly fast to can give an adrenaline surge like no other.

Day trading may likewise furnish you with preferable influence over holding positions overnight (as in swing trading). At the hour of this composition, day trading stocks can furnish you with 4:1 use as long as you meet certain criteria.

Day trading additionally furnishes you with another sort of influence, which is that since you're trading so much of the time, you can utilize a similar capital in your record to make numerous exchanges a brief timeframe.

Probably the best advantage of day trading is that you maintain a strategic distance from the medium-term hazard. Medium-term hazard alludes to the way that when you hold a situation overnight, your money is presented to major startling moves while the market is shut and you're resting. Such startling sensational moves might be brought about off guard, political, or military news in your nation or another.

These sensational moves medium-term might be brought about by genuinely awful news, or just gossipy tidbits, or a difference in feeling about a stock, division, or industry. These moves appear as holes — altogether unexpected opening costs in comparison to where the markets shut the prior day — on your outline and can hop your quits, giving an immense misfortune to you when you get up the following morning.

A stop is a request you spot to be filled at a specific cost if the market betrays your exchange; hopping your stops happens when the market holes to a value that is past where you put in your stop request.

A stop is frequently called a defensive stop since it's utilized as a defensive measure with the expectation of setting the level at which you need to leave an exchange that is not going your direction. Right now, endeavoring to restrain your hazard in the exchange.

There are various advantages to day trading. Probably the greatest advantage is it permits a sufficient chance to learn it. Learn, test, and watch your trading procedure with our assistance. You can do this from the solace of your own home – there's no requirement for office gear, decorations, or a chief. On the off chance that you have the control, you can work effectively in an agreeable, well-known condition. We'll additionally assist you with accomplishing steadiness via preparing you to rehearse sound trading standards and venture strategies. With our assistance, you can accomplish a quick profit for your speculation.

Advantages of Day Trading

If you need to trade stocks and hoping to turn into a day trader, it's critical to comprehend what you're getting yourself into and the advantages and the disadvantages. So in the event that you need to change and turn into a swing trader, at that point, you'll, in any event, know the purpose for it.

Most importantly, a day trader is somebody that holds stock or position, not exactly a day, which is 6 ½ hours, since the trading day last 6 ½ hours. So you can hold it for 20 minutes, you can hold it for 60 minutes, you can hold it for five hours.

It's thoroughly up to you; you can hold if for a moment. It doesn't make a difference. However, it's not exactly an entire day. That is the thing that a day trader is, and that is their specialty, whereas a swing trader holds a situation for numerous days, two, three days, seven days, a month. For longer-term positions.

How about we talk about the advantages behind being a day trader. Bit of leeway number one is that a day trader has no medium-term hazard on holes or income since you're hundred percent money before the day's over. The subsequent thing is that your income compound quicker, so in case you're bringing in money each and every day, you're ready to utilize the money that you produced using the earlier day to place into the following trading day.

It permits you to truly quicken your exacerbating income over and over. This is one of the extraordinary attractions to individuals for day trading is on the grounds that it resembles brisk money. Presently additionally behind day trading, there's greater energy. This is regularly a passionate state, and a ton of beginner traders are truly pulled in today's trading since they find a workable pace account fluctuating here and there all over. Furthermore, you get actually sincerely attached to it; it resembles wow my benefit's going up. Or on the other hand, wow, this truly sucks, my benefits going down. There is that surge of the feelings that are going on yet again like I said that is ordinarily for fledgling or beginners, and it is anything but a decent method to be, in case you're hoping to exchange.

In the event that effective, the prizes of day trading can far surpass the risks. Day trading requires order and time management. However, it additionally bears a person to make their own hours without a chief or manager remaining over their back. What's more, notwithstanding the measure of money an individual can make structure the solace of their own home, day trading offers people numerous advantages they won't experience in the more customary types of trading stocks and other monetary instruments.

Day Trading Risks

Day trading, as recently referenced, can be dangerous. Basically, day traders ought not to hazard the money that they can't bear to lose. Once more, it is your money on the line, not a company's, so you should be certain you feel good with your insight into the market. Hence, it is basic that you have the control and hard-working attitude to oversee this undertaking; and you should be your own manager. You have to have an inside arrangement of checks and equalization to ensure you don't face an excessive number of challenges or start to overtrade. You have to figure out how to assume a misfortune, since misfortunes will happen, particularly toward the starting stages. The compensations of day trading are high, yet so are the risks.

Plausibility of Large Losses

Contingent upon the choices made during the day, a trader could find hundreds to thousands of dollars. You ought to be set up to endure extreme monetary misfortunes; this is a piece of the procedure.

Numerous beginner day traders endure serious money related misfortunes in their first long stretches of trading, and some don't remain in the game long enough to see a benefit. Most day traders submit to a significant ideology: just hazard the money you can bear to lose.

Requests of Day Trading

Day trading requires time and consideration paid to the markets, and their patterns and everyday exercises. A ton of centers must be placed into the market hours, which requires a lot of time before the PC screen prepared to execute an exchange immediately. Notwithstanding the time responsibility, day trading requires a ton of concentrate outside of your trading hours. A concentrated measure of information is required so as to be fruitful at this profoundly requesting calling.

Stress

Stress is a piece of consistently trading work. This isn't just because of the conceivable outcomes of huge misfortunes, yet additionally on account of the possibility that a ton of people in the ventures field sees it as betting.

Like watching a games group you wager on, day trading can cause elevated levels of pressure and uneasiness sitting tight at a stock's cost. Also, the activity necessitates that you settle on fast choices concerning the obtaining or selling of protections, with escalated time imperatives.

Overtrading

Overtrading can come in two structures: 1. facing an excessive number of challenges/making such a large number of dangerous exchanges, and 2. trading too huge offers. Starting day traders regularly get overpowered with the quick pace of day trading and let their feelings, rather than their insight and investigation, settle on the choices for them.

Stock Trade Commissions

Albeit numerous day traders manage direct access intermediaries and numerous online day trading locales offer low commissions, it is conceivable that commissions will meddle with your capacity to make a genuine benefit. Because of the fast style of trading, and the huge volume of exchanges (each exchange conveys with it a commission), a great deal of money from your benefits – or out of your pocket – will go toward commissions.

Model: For a $10 commission for each exchange, a speedy purchase and sell exchange would cost $20. This would be 20% of a $100 benefit or 10% of a $200 benefit.

Obtaining Money

Day traders depend intensely on obtained money or purchasing stocks on edge (guarantee held to cover the danger of the exchange). Acquiring money to exchange stocks consistently holds a few risks. Day traders use the influence (acquiring money to enhance existing assets for a more prominent return) of obtained money to expand returns. If not fruitful, this could prompt the trader losing enormous totals of money and conceivably an accumulation of obligation. This is the reason it is critical to know about the essentials of day trading before wandering into the field.

Understanding Market Trends

The focal point of a day trader's day is sitting before a PC screen and looking for stocks that have some development. They will, in general, follow a stock's momentum and make a speedy exchange before it changes course. Since day traders don't know without a doubt how a stock will move, it is significant that they know about market patterns and money related and speculation examination. Among these significant patterns and apparatuses of investigation are technical examination, market and venture graphs, and theory. In the event that this information is missing structure a day trader's expertise base, at that point, this undertaking turns out to be considerably less secure than it as of now is.

Limitations

Under the standards of NYSE and NASD, clients who are esteemed "design day traders" must-have in any event $25,000 in their records and can just exchange edge accounts. Some different limitations can apply to day traders. Counsel the SEC (Securities and Exchanges Commission) site for additional, critical data.

Out-of-Pocket Expenses

Beginning as a day trader can cost a great deal of money out of pocket. It might be said; you would already be able to start your day trading profession in the red. These costs can include programming (and equipment), commissions, manuals, and different assets. It is critical to building up a spending limit for these out-of-pocket costs before entering the field of day trading. These costs could increment once you push ahead in your day trading profession.

Record Keeping and Taxes

As a day trader, you are ready to go for yourself. Thus, notwithstanding being the chief, you are likewise the bookkeeper, the full-time bookkeeper at that. You should know about exchanges made and money earned, and each April, it will be your obligation to check those records to appropriately give Uncle Sam his offer. Some time or other traders, contingent upon pay, are dependent upon independent work charges.

Innovation

Basically, power blackouts, programming/equipment issues, disturbed web associations. It could occur.

Chapter 3 Psychology and Mindset

Day Trading, like any other form of investment, is subject to influence from human emotion and psychological impact. Whenever money or capital is in play, people tend to take matters rather personally because of the inevitable consequence of the hope that comes along with the promise of significant returns. People will strive to make money while at the same time, avoid circumstances that may cause them to lose their capital. It is from this zerosum mentality that the influence of psychology or emotions may creep into a sensible mindset. Such control takes over every aspect of the Day Trading instincts that you learned over time.

Your knowledge goes out of the window when a situation that triggers your psychological response arises. A high degree of counterproductivity thus ensues. It, eventually, leads to the dismissal of logical decisions in favor of hunches as well as the need to chase after fleeting profits and cover your previous losses. For you to manage your Day Trading expertise through challenging scenarios, you need to look out for emotions that alter your reasoning capability adversely. Try to improve and nurture a productive mindset, while at the same time, avoid promoting a mental culture that justifies negativity falsely. The following few behaviors and traits are central to your particular mindset whenever you decide to participate in Day Trading:

Do Not Rationalize Your Trading Errors

This mindset t is one of the leading obstacles to the progress and eventual success of your Day Trading endeavors. You are often prone to justify any trading mistakes that you make to the detriment of moving forward. For instance, you get an entry into a particularly promising trade deal later than necessary in spite of your much earlier knowledge of its potential for profitability. The delay causes you to miss an excellent opportunity at the previous entry point. However, you decide to justify this misstep by convincing yourself of your preference for trading late over missing the same deal entirely.

The downside to such delays is often a faulty sense of size estimation in taking your trading position. Hence, the resulting increased exposure to financial risk you become disadvantaged by. Beware of your procrastination when it comes to productive openings that are currently available in Day Trading. If you possess this tendency, consider getting rid of it as soon as possible before it costs you a lot more capital in the long run. In case you are not prone to the frequent postponement of your responsibilities to a later date, be alert for the development of this mentality with the trading company that you keep. You can quickly become influenced by the kind of traders from whom you seek advice on more complex trading strategies. When present, stockbrokers affect your trading ethos, as well.

Poor trading etiquette from these external sources will rub off on you and vice versa. Try to keep the company of well-known responsible trading partners and stockbrokers when the need arises. Another rationalization scenario involves a run of profitable results. Based on a series of trade deals that made you successive returns, you begin to convince your brain of your seemingly high intelligence. This false belief in your skills may lead you to overestimate your trading expertise. Before long, you may start engaging in Day Trading on a hunch rather than apply logic to your decisions. You stop referring to your trusted trading plan and jump into many trading opportunities haphazardly. After a while, these instances of carelessness and trading arrogance will catch up with you because they always inevitably do. Your chances of plunging into a financial disaster go up.

With your eventual financial ruin come the cases of psychological meltdown leading to a negative feedback loop. A wrong decision from your misplaced sense of conceitedness will invariably lead to high-risk exposure. As a result, you suffer significant losses eventually, and consequently, your emotional health suffers, causing you to spiral into a state of depression. This loop is often self-propagating, meaning that it feeds onto itself. Bad decisions lead to adverse outcomes and a fragile mindset, which, in turn, is prone to make more bad decisions, and the loop goes on and on. Keep in mind that in Day Trading, such a feedback loop is often disastrous. All these adverse effects arise from your initial false sense of justification for a wrong deed.

Beware of Your Trading Decisions

This advice is so apparent that it sounds redundant when mentioned. However, decisions are typically the product of your reasoning and judgment at a particular moment. When it comes to decisions on Day Trading, psychological influence is often a determining factor in the process. Keeping your wits about you is very crucial, especially when everything seems to be out of control. You need to realize that every trade has its ups and downs and how you deal with the challenging times is often more consequential. Try to maintain a logical mindset when making Day Trading choices from a variety of bad options. When it seems that an imminent financial downturn is inevitable, the extent of your loss becomes essential. In this case, you will need to make a sensible decision on the degree of losing margins that you can tolerate adequately.

At this point, you are probably in a state of so many overwhelming emotions that your foggy mental faculties become clouded. An expected human response is to run away from danger, naturally, but in certain situations, fleeing may not be an option. A reflex in a trading scenario often leads to an impulsive decision. Such a choice is, in turn, typically not well thought or deliberative. You should confront your unfavorable circumstances head-on and attempt to fix the situation, however hopeless. This sense of perseverance is usually the essence of most trading excursions, especially when the times become financially rough. Going through the loss of some capital and other Day Trading challenges is often a painful experience that can lead to illogical decisions.

Always remember to uphold vigilance and adhere strictly to the guidelines in your trading plan when confronted with obstacles during your trades. The trading plan usually has instructions on how to handle these seemingly desperate situations. In addition, the prior preparation of any trading guide is generally free of emotional or psychological influence; hence, you can rely on it to maintain neutrality. Also, beware of making trading resolutions when going through a phase with a foul mood. Such conclusions are bound to lead you into a financial catastrophe, especially if you are not careful. Learn to put off the verdict to a time when you can resume logical thinking. When you make any rash decision, it can only result in your further exposure to even more risk.

Keep Your Emotions in Check

Learn to stick to a Day Trading system and method that you trust. Such a strategy may be one that has a history of always making significant returns. Once you master and fully grasp how to apply a specific approach to your trading deals, try to fine-tune it to your preference based on your ultimate objectives. Afterward, stick to this tried, practiced, and tested system in all your searches for valid trade deals. On some days, the stock market may be slow with a low volume of trade. The volatility in such a case is often negligible. However, due to an unchecked emotional influence, you develop a sense of greed or lust for profits.

The desire for benefits on a slow day is common. It leads to the urge to trade on anything to make a small profit. In this situation, you will move from Day Trading into gambling. Trading requires a logical mindset on your part with a lack of psychological attachment whatsoever. Gambling is a consequence of emotional and mental factors running amok in your Day Trading system. If a particular trading style worked on multiple times in the past, teach your brain to consider it. Your trusted trading system will indicate a lack of valid trade opportunities on a specific slow market day. In this case, curb your emotions, desires, and urges to chase a quick profit; however strong they seem.

You should never allow yourself to resort to gambling under any circumstances. Gambling is detrimental to healthy and responsible Day Trading behavior. The risk exposure exponentially rises when you grow accustomed to the desire for profits. If a given day of trading is unfavorable, you should not take part in invalid and unworthy deals. In addition, you should only trade on verifiable opportunities. At certain times, you may experience a series of successive returns in a relatively short period. Learn to know when to stop and how to curb your lust for wanting more returns. Trust your system to trade only on valid deals; however, multiple opportunities are available. An emotion that goes unmonitored in such situations is the greed for more profit.

You convince yourself psychologically that the various deals could be a sign of your lucky day. This mentality in a false belief is wrong, and you need to be aware of it. Your psychology can play deceitful tricks on your logical mind leading to high-risk trading deals. You must realize that in Day Trading, it is almost impossible to get more returns out of a system than what the stock market offers. Emotional corruption also comes into play in a scenario where you bite off more than you can chew.

The greed for substantial amounts of returns may cause you to take highrisk trading positions for a chance at quick profits. However, you must remember that profits and losses are both possible outcomes from a Day Trading session. Therefore, you need to learn to trade in amounts that you can afford to lose. After all, Day Trading involves taking a chance based on a speculative position. You should practice trading in small amounts of money within the confines of low-risk deals. In this case, a potential loss may not be as damaging as the earlier high-risk trading position driven by greed. Eliminate the role of emotions in Day Trading and learn to accept the uncertainty of an unknown future outcome.

Be Patient When Trading

Patience is a crucial trait to have when you take part in Day Trading due to the upswings and downward trends in stock prices. It can become challenging to identify the right entry or exit point for a particular trading opportunity, given the fluctuating nature of a volatile market. However, when you master the art of being patient and studying the trade intently, you can come up with a winning strategy. Having a planned approach is essential, and you should prepare one before engaging in any Day Trading. Often, most seasoned traders include trading strategies for different market conditions in their trading plans. Hence, when making your trading plan, consider incorporating a trading strategy within it.

If unsure of how to proceed, you can always seek the assistance of qualified stockbrokers. They have the experience of encountering various Day Trading scenarios in the real world. If trustworthy, they could provide you with invaluable insights on coming up with a proper strategy. Now it is up to you to stick to the plan in every session in which you participate. Patience demands that you pay attention to the planned strategy and ignore any attractive distractions when trading. For instance, a brief upswing from a potential price action breakout may be misleading. It might cause you to falsely believe that the stock price is about to pick momentum and keep rising on the chart.

However, as attractive as this scenario might be, a sense of diligent patience demands that you ignore it and refer to your strategy. Upon referral to your trading plan strategy, you may encounter the concept of false breakouts. You also learn that these false upswings in trend usually follow a prolonged period of price consolidated. As a result, your patience allows you to evade a potentially wrong entry point to a trading position. You are also able to pick the right exit point from a particular trading session based on strategic patience. The price action chart acts merely as a guide for your trading actions and not the determining factor.

WHAT ARE THE RIGHT REQUIREMENTS FOR DAY TRADING

Beginning day to day exchange isn't a choice to be trifled with. It is conceivable to be effective and win decent living trading just a couple of hours out of every day, except that objective is numerous months away for individuals simply beginning. The primary year is intense; there are heaps of good and bad times, and your first practical objective ought to be essentially not to lose everything. On the off chance that you, despite everything, need to begin day trading, there are five things you have to do so as to put yourself in the correct way.

1. Make or Learn a Strategy

Day trading isn't something to do spontaneously. It requires a sound and practiced strategy that gives you a factual edge on each exchange you make.

- How would you get into an exchange?
- How would you get over both winning and losing exchanges)?
- How much would you chance on the exchange, and what position size would you take (what number of portions of stock, loads of money, or fates contracts)?

- After choosing this, what are the chances the exchange will be beneficial? Furthermore, in the event that you take comparative kinds of exchanges multiple times, what propensities does your strategy appear?

The best way to respond to these inquiries is by actualizing a similar technique again and again and observing the outcomes. You can make a strategy by discovering propensities in the everyday value activity of a benefit, or you can take in a strategy from another person.

2. Practice a Lot

Rehearsing is key in day trading. To be acceptable at a game, you practice. Indeed, even at the lowest pay permitted by law work, the manager, for the most part, makes you practice what you should do before you do it seriously. With a great many your well-deserved dollars in question, practice is critical. However, new day traders once in a while practice.

You practice in a demo account before you chance a solitary genuine dollar. Do so systematically, trading your made or learned strategy again and again. What you will discover is that no two exchanges are ever precisely the equivalent. Today might be unstable, while tomorrow is steady. Today is drifting, while tomorrow is extending. If you don't rehearse, you may miss exchange flags or be slanted to make exchanges that aren't a piece of your strategy.

Practice just the strategy you are taking a shot at. Realize it well, and impeccable it. When you include the weight of trading genuine capital, you would prefer not to, in any case, be pondering whether you should take an exchange or not.

Practice until you have been gainful in a demo represents a while. At exactly that point, think about opening a live record with genuine capital.

3. Know the Capital Requirements

Funding to a day trader resembles stock to a storekeeper. You need it to work, and the amount you have—and how you oversee it—will decide your salary.

You legitimately need like $25,000 to begin day trading stocks to give yourself a cushion, store in any event $30,000. In the event that you enter and leave stock situations around the same time with under $25,000, your record will be hailed, and you risk losing your trading privileges.1

Forex day trading doesn't have a lawful least, however, start with at any rate $500. Not as much as that, and you're restricted on the number of exchanges you can take. In the event that you need to create a month to month pay that merits pulling back, start with $5,000 or more.

Today exchange fates, start with at any rate $2,500. However, $7,500 to $10,000 is better. A few agreements cost more to exchange than others. However, in the event that you intend to exchange the normal E-small S&P 500, that scope of capital will get the job done.

Making a pay is conceivable, however difficult, on these suggested store sums.

4. Think about Goals and Constraints

Before you put the time in making or learning and afterward rehearsing a day trading strategy, think about your objectives and requirements.

- Do you have enough funding to do the exchange? If not, hold up until you do. Meanwhile, you can keep rehearsing your strategy.

- Becoming reliably gainful takes a half year to a year while rehearsing a few hours every day. It will take longer in the event that you do it just discontinuously. Is it true that you will be placed in that measure of time?

- Once you are trading life, would you be able to focus on trading a few hours per day, representing your activity and different duties?

- You shouldn't surrender your activity until your trading benefits supplant your salary. In this manner, given your different duties, what time of day would you be able to exchange? Is your strategy intended for that season of the day? Your strategy needs to accommodate your life.

- Are you day trading since you need to leave your place of employment? You will probably need to exchange for a year or more to arrive at where you can supplant your pay by day trading.

Consider every one of these inquiries before investing a great deal of time or money in figuring out how today's exchange.

5. Pick a Broker

While you are rehearsing and creating strategies, pick an intermediary. This might be a similar merchant you open a demo account with, or it might be another. Picking your agent is the greatest "exchange" you will make since you are confiding in them with the entirety of your capital. Search for a representative who offsets incredible execution with client support, notoriety, and serious charges

CONTROLLED RISK AND RETURN RATIO IN DAY TRADING

What Is the Risk/Reward Ratio?

The hazard/reward proportion denotes the forthcoming prize an investor can procure. For each dollar, the individual in question risks on a venture. Numerous investors use hazard/reward proportions to look at the normal returns of speculation with the measure of hazard they should attempt to procure these profits. Think about the accompanying model: a venture with a hazard reward proportion of 1:7 proposes that an investor is happy to chance $1, for the possibility of winning $7. Then again, a hazard/reward proportion of 1:3 signs that an investor ought to hope to contribute $1, for the possibility of gaining $3 on his speculation.

Traders regularly utilize this way to deal with a plan which exchanges to take, and the proportion is determined by partitioning the sum a trader stands to lose if the cost of an advantage moves a startling way (the hazard) by the measure of benefit the trader expects to have made when the position is shut (the Reward).

- The hazard/reward proportion is utilized by traders to deal with their capital and danger of misfortune during trading.

- The proportion surveys the normal return and danger of a given exchange.

- A great hazard reward proportion will, in general, be anything more prominent than 1 of every 3.

How the Risk/Reward Ratio Works

The hazard/reward proportion is frequently utilized as a measure when trading singular stocks. The ideal hazard/reward proportion generally contrasts among different trading strategies. Some experimentation techniques are generally required to figure out which proportion is best for a given trading strategy, and numerous investors have a pre-indicated chance/reward proportion for their speculations.

By and large, market strategists locate the perfect hazard/reward proportion for their ventures to be roughly 1:3, or three units of anticipated return for each one unit of extra hazard. Investors can oversee chance/reward all the more legitimately using stop-misfortune requests and subordinates, for example, put alternatives.

What Does the Risk/Reward Ratio Tell You?

The hazard/reward proportion assists investors in dealing with their danger of losing money on exchanges. Regardless of whether a trader has some gainful exchanges, he will lose money after some time if his success rate is beneath half. The hazard/reward proportion gauges the distinction between an exchange passage point to a stop-misfortune and a sell or take-benefit request. Looking at these two gives the proportion of benefit to misfortune, or compensation to chance.

Investors frequently use stop-misfortune orders when trading singular stocks to help limit misfortunes and legitimately deal with their speculations with a hazard/reward center. A stop-misfortune request is a trading trigger set on a stock that computerizes the selling of the stock from a portfolio if the stock arrives at a predetermined low. Investors can naturally set stop-misfortune arranges through money market funds, and ordinarily don't require extreme extra trading costs.

Case of the Risk/Reward Ratio being used

Think about this model: A trader buys 100 portions of XYZ Company at $20 and submits a stop-misfortune request at $15 to guarantee that misfortunes won't surpass $500. Additionally, expect that this trader accepts that the cost of XYZ will reach $30 in the following hardly any months. Right now, the trader is happy to chance $5 per offer to make a normal return of $10 per share subsequent to shutting the position. Since the trader stands to make twofold the sum that she has gambled, she would be said to have a 1:2 hazard/reward proportion on that specific exchange. Subsidiaries agreements, for example, put contracts, which give their proprietors the option to sell the fundamental resource at a predefined cost, can be utilized to comparable impact.

In the event that a progressive preservationist investor looks for a 1:5 hazard/reward proportion for a predetermined venture (five units of anticipated return for each extra unit of hazard), at that point, he can utilize the stop-misfortune request to modify the hazard/reward proportion to his own particular. Right now, the trading model noted above, and if an investor has a 1:5 hazard/reward proportion required for his speculation, he will set the stop-misfortune request at $18 rather than $15—that is, he is more hazard disinclined.

Chapter 4 Tools of the Trade

The main tools you'll need for day trading are an online broker and an order execution platform. It goes without saying that you'll also need a very good internet connection and a computer on which to execute your trades on the platform. And if you're not part of a day trading community yet, you'll also need a stock scanner.

The Broker

You'll need a very good broker, who'll be your access to the securities market you plan to day trade in, e.g., the stock market. Take note that your broker can't just be good: it has to be very good. Why?

Since you can't access the stock market or other securities markets directly, you'll need to go through a broker. Even if you choose your SIPs correctly, you can still lose money in your trades if your broker's slow to execute your order at your target price or if their system suffers from frequent glitches.

It can be challenging to choose a broker because there are many of them out there. Some offer top service but are expensive while some charge very low fees but their service is crappy. Worse, some are both expensive and crappy! To help you narrow down your choices to quality brokers, I'll provide a list of really good ones at the end of this book in the appendix.

Minimum Equity Requirement

The United States Securities and Exchange Commission (SEC) and the Financial Industry Regulatory Authority (FINRA) enforce rules on people who day trade. They use the term Pattern Day Trader to qualify those who can engage in day trading with stock brokerage firms operating in the United States.

The qualify pattern day traders as those who day trades, i.e., takes and closes positions within the same day, at least four times in the last five business days. The SEC and FINRA require that pattern day traders must have a minimum equity balance of $25,000 in their brokerage account before they day trade. When the equity balance falls below this amount for one reason or another, brokers are compelled to prohibit pattern day traders from executing new day trades until they're able to bring their equity back up to at least $25,000.

Many newbie day traders, especially those who only have this minimum amount, look at this rule as more of a hindrance to day trading glory rather than a protective fence against day trading tragedies. They don't realize that it's mean to keep them from taking excessive day trading risks that can easily wipe out their trading capitals in a jiffy because of their brokers' commissions and fees.

While this rule is the minimum requirement under the law, many brokers and dealers may use a stricter definition of a pattern day trader for purposes of transacting with them. The best thing to do is to clarify this minimum equity requirement with your chosen broker to avoid confusion later on.

If you can't afford the $25,000 minimum equity requirement for day trading, you can opt to trade with an offshore broker instead. They're brokerage firms that operate outside the United States such as Capital Markets Elite Group

Limited, which operates out of Trinidad and Tobago. Because these brokers operate outside the jurisdiction of FINRA, they're not subject to the pattern day trader rule. This means you're also not subject to the same minimum amount.

But before you think of trading with offshore brokers, keep in mind that these brokers are beyond the juridical reach of the SEC and FINRA. This means if anything goes wrong, you can't count on the Federal Government to help you out. If you really want to use them to avoid the pattern day trader rule, just make sure to limit the amount of day trading equity you'll place with such brokers to an amount that you're comfortable risking or losing.

Direct-Access and Conventional Brokers

Conventional brokers normally reroute their customers' orders, including yours, to other firms through some sort of pre-agreed upon order processing scheme. Thus, executing your orders through conventional brokers involve more steps and can take significantly more time. And when it comes to day trading, speed is essential.

Conventional brokers are often referred to as full-service brokers because they tend to provide customers with other services such as market research and investment advice, among others. Because of these "extras", their commissions and fees are usually much higher than direct-access brokers. Conventional or full-service brokers are ideal for long-term investors and swing traders because they're not as particular with the speed of trade executions as day traders are.

Compared to full-service or conventional brokers, direct-access brokers focus more on the speed of trade executions than research and advisory services. And because they often skip the extra services to focus on providing fast and easy access to the stock market, they charge less commissions and fees. This has earned many of them the alias "discount brokers".

Direct-access brokers use very powerful computer programs and provide customers online platforms through which they can directly trade the stock market, whether it's the NASDAQ or the NYSE. And while they provide the necessary trade execution speeds required in day trading, they're not perfect and they have their share of challenges.

One such challenge is the imposition of monthly trading volume quotas. If you fail to meet their minimum monthly trading volume, they'll charge you an "inactivity fee", which often serves as their minimum monthly commission from your and all their other clients' accounts. However, not all discount brokerage firms impose inactivity fees.

Another challenge particular to direct-access brokers concerns newbie day traders, i.e., familiarity with direct-access trading. With conventional brokers, all a newbie trader needs to do is tell their broker the details of their orders and the broker will be the one to take care of all things related to executing their orders in the market. With direct-access brokers, the day trader him or herself executes the orders through the broker's online platform or software.

This can be quite challenging for newbie day traders because apart from choosing their SIPs, they also need to know how to execute their orders on the platform properly. But since day trading is a more sophisticated form of stock market trading, the chances are high that newbie day traders have enough experience with direct-access trading already.

But just in case your new to both direct-access brokerage trading and day trading, your best bet would be to practice on a broker's trading simulator before you even consider opening and trading a real account with that broker. That way, you'll have one less thing to think about when you finally start to day trade.

The Trading Platform

A trading platform pertains to the computer program or software that you'll use to day trade. This is different from the direct-access broker itself, but many traders make the mistake of thinking they're one and the same.

The trading platform is what you'll use to send your orders to the stock exchange, which the direct-access broker will clear on your behalf. While it's different from the direct-access brokers, it's not unusual for such brokers to develop and have their clients use their own proprietary trading platforms to trade stocks in the exchange.

The number and quality of the features of trading platforms influence the price direct-access brokers charge their clients for their services. The more features a platform has, the higher the commissions and fees may be and vice versa.

A very important feature that you should look for in a trading platform are Hotkeys. Without them, you may not be able to execute trades fast enough to make them profitable. Considering that day trading focuses on stocks with relatively high volatility, being a second or two late can spell the difference of taking and closing positions at the ideal prices and missing out on profitable day trading opportunities.

Real Time Market Data

Unlike long-term investors and swing traders who only need end-of-day price data that's available for free online, day traders need real time data as the trading day unfolds because they need to get in and out of positions within a matter of hours, minutes, or even seconds. And unfortunately, access to real time intraday price data isn't free and you'll need to pay monthly fees to your direct-access broker or the platform owner (if different from the brokerage firm) for them. Just ask your direct-access broker for details on their monthly fees for access to real time day trading data.

Two of the most basic types of data that you'll need to look at as a day trader are the bid and ask prices. The bid prices are the prices at which other traders and investors are willing to buy a particular stock. The ask prices are the prices at which other traders and investors are willing to sell a particular stock.

The bid and ask prices are arranged such that the best price is at the top. The best bid price is the highest one, i.e., the best price for sellers is the highest price at which buyers are willing to buy. The best ask price, on the other hand, is the lowest price at which sellers are willing to sell. It's considered the best price from the perspective of buyers. Bid and ask prices also indicate the number of shares that other traders and investors are willing to buy or sell them at specific prices.

The bid prices are usually listed on the left side while the ask prices are usually listed on the right such that the best bid and ask prices are right beside each other. If you want to execute your buy orders immediately, you "buy up" the best ask price. If you want to immediately execute your sell orders, "sell down" at the best bid price.

The Day Trading Orders

The three most important types of day trading orders are market, limit, and marketable limit orders.

Market orders refer to orders to buy or sell stocks at their current market prices for immediate execution. If you remember from earlier, these refer to buying up at the best current ask price or selling down at the best bid price.

Depending on market conditions and subsequent price movements during the day, market orders may be the worst or best prices to trade in. For example, if you send a market order to sell when the bid-ask prices are $1.00-$1.05 and the by the time your order hits the market, the bid-ask prices shift to $0.95-$1.01, your sell order will be done at $0.95. In this example, your sell proceeds get cut by a minimum of five cents multiplied by the number of shares you sold.

On the other hand, let's say you sent a buy market order when the current bid-ask prices are $1.10-$1.15. If the bid-ask prices change to $1.12-$1.17

by the time your market order reaches the market, you'll end up paying $0.02 cents more for every share of that stock.

Only market makers and professional traders with a lot of day trading expertise and experience can benefit from market orders. For retail day traders like you and I, we should avoid market orders as much as possible. Why?

Hardware

You must avoid using wireless or Bluetooth keyboards and mice for day trading. Why? Here are some things that can happen with wireless keyboards and mice that can negatively impact your day trading activities:

They put you at risk of getting low on power or getting completely drained at the height of your day trading activities, which will immobilize you from day trading until you're able to switch to another keyboard and put you at risk of missing out on key prices;

They can erroneously execute key strokes multiple times, particularly when low in power; and

They can fail to send orders if the signal's interrupted by low power or other signal interruptions.

Aside from sticking to wired keyboards and mice for your trading, make sure you have a set of backups in case something happens, like spilling drinks on them. Better safe than sorry.

Stock Pick Scanners and Watchlists

Because there are thousands of stocks that are eligible for day trading every single trading day, it's impossible to manually scan the market for SIPs fast enough to make timely day trades. That's why you'll need to use a marketscanning software to short list your day trading choices. One of the most popular market-scanning software in the market today that you can consider for your day trading activities is Trade Ideas at www.tradeideas.com.

Day Trading Community

No man (or woman, to be more gender-sensitive) is an island, as the saying goes. This includes day traders.

Day trading can be overwhelming for newbies and one of the best ways that you can more easily navigate through it is by joining a community of day traders. There, you can find technical, intellectual, and dare I say even emotional support as you begin traversing the road less traveled called day trading. You can glean useful pieces of day trading information such as which stocks are about to be in day trading play and new day trading methods and tactics, among others.

Get Your Education

You need to make sure you are educated on your topic. You want to treat day trading as your new career. Therefore, you should make sure that you have researched your topic and consider yourself an expert on day trading. Of course, there are lessons that you are going to learn naturally as you start day trading. Experienced traders believe that people should take about three to four months and practice with simulators before practicing with money.

Build Your Business Plan

You need to have a business plan. One of the biggest factors to remember when you are getting into day trading is you must treat it like any other serious career choice. With any business you would start up and get into, you will have a business plan. You need to make sure your education is part of your business plan (for example, any classes you are planning on taking). You also must make sure your schedule, the tools you will use, platforms, technology, software, and anything else incorporated in your business is a part of your business plan.

Another thing to remember when creating your business plan is to look at every single detail. You do not want to miss something or think it is fine to skip over anything. On top of this, you want to make sure that you look at your business plan often, even after you start trading. In fact, it is best if you look at your business plan at least once a month, if not more.

Make Sure You Have the Right Supplies

You will want to make sure that you find a system of support from a community of traders, have high-speed internet service, a great platform which supports hotkeys, a scanner which will help you find the right stocks to trade, and the best broker. You will also want to make sure that you can financially handle the bills that will become a part of your new day trading career. These bills can include leases and licenses for software, your monthly internet bill, electricity bill, your broker's commission, and any platform costs. Furthermore, you will probably want to become a part of an online community, a practice that has several benefits I will discuss later in his book, and bear in mind that these communities often have subscriptions.

Have Enough Cash

You will need to make sure that you have enough cash, which is often referred to as startup capital. Like any other business, you will want to make sure you can afford to take on day trading. However, you will not only need money when you start investing, you will also need money to make sure that you can afford the bills and technology that goes into day trading, as mentioned earlier.

Making sure you have enough finances is an important step because one of the main reasons why most day traders lose their money or go bankrupt is because they didn't have enough startup capital. If you need to hold off on starting up your day trading career for a couple of months or more in order to make sure you have enough capital, that is okay. As the old saying goes, it is better to be safe than sorry. You don't want to find yourself thinking of ways to cut back in order to save your money for investing. For example, it is a bad idea to decide not to go forth with any classes or day-trading community subscriptions over financial concerns, as these are incredibly important. If you start cutting back on the tools that can help you become a successful day trader, you can easily find yourself in a downward spiral. This can cause you not only to lose more money but also cause you a lot of stress and emotions within trading, which can cause more problems within your investing career by impairing your ability to make quick decisions based on logical analysis. If you are not prepared, you are more likely to make mistakes.

THE BEST STRATEGIES AND TECHNIQUES TO START WITH DAY TRADING

STRATEGIES

Day trading strategies are basic when you are hoping to profit by visit, little value developments. A steady, compelling strategy depends on top to bottom technical examination, using graphs, indicators, and examples to foresee future value developments. This page will offer you a careful reprieve down of beginner trading strategies, working as far as possible up to cutting edge, computerized, and even resource explicit strategies.

It will likewise layout some local contrasts to know about, just as pointing you toward some valuable assets. At last, however, you'll have to discover a day trading strategy that suits your particular trading style and prerequisites.

Likewise, guarantee your decision of intermediary suits strategy based day trading. You will need things like;

- Excellent exchange execution speed,
- Price activity information (+ Level 2 if conceivable)
- Ability to exchange direct from diagrams,
- Trade robotization,
- Stop misfortunes and take benefit orders
- Etc and so forth.

Trading Strategies for Beginners

Before you get hindered in an unpredictable universe of exceptionally technical indicators, center around the nuts and bolts of a basic day trading strategy. Many wrongly think you need an exceptionally muddled strategy to succeed intraday, yet frequently the more clear, the more powerful.

The Basics

Consolidate the priceless components underneath your strategy.

- Money management – Before you start, plunk down and choose the amount you're willing to hazard. Remember, best traders won't put over 2% of their capital at risk per exchange. You need to set yourself up for certain misfortunes on the off chance that you need to associate with when the successes begin coming in.

- Time management – Don't hope to make a fortune in the event that you just assign an hour or two every day to trading. You have to continually screen the markets and be vigilant for exchange openings.

- Start little – Whilst you're finding your feet, adhere to a limit of three stocks during a solitary day.

- Education – Understanding market complexities isn't sufficient, and you additionally need to remain educated. Ensure you keep awake to date with market news and any occasions that will affect your advantage, for example, a move in a financial arrangement. You can discover an abundance of online money related and business assets that will keep you aware of everything.

- Consistency – It's difficult than it hopes to keep feelings under control when you're five espressos, and you've been gazing at the screen for quite a long time. You have to let calculation, rationale, and your strategy direct you, not nerves, dread, or insatiability.

- Timing – The market will be unstable when it opens every day, and keeping in mind that accomplished day traders might have the option to peruse the examples and benefit, you ought to await your opportunity. So keep down for the first 15 minutes, you've despite everything advanced hours beyond.

- Demo Account – An unquestionable requirement have device for any novice yet, in addition, the best spot to backtest or explore different avenues regarding new, or refined, strategies for cutting edge traders. Many demo accounts are boundless, so not time-limited.

5 Day Trading Strategies

1. Breakout

Breakout strategies base on when the cost clears a predefined level on your graph, with expanded volume. The breakout trader goes into a long situation after the benefit or security breaks above the opposition. On the other hand, you enter a short position once the stock breaks beneath help.

After an advantage or security exchanges past the predetermined cost boundary, volatility normally increments, and costs will frequently slant toward the breakout.

You have to identify the correct instrument to exchange. While doing this, remember the advantage's help and opposition levels. The more every now and again the cost has hit these focuses, the more approved and significant they become.

This part is pleasant and clear. Costs set to close or more obstruction levels require a bearish position. Costs set to close, and beneath a help, level needs a bullish position.

Plan your ways out

Utilize the benefit's ongoing exhibition to set up a sensible value target. Utilizing graph examples will make this procedure much increasingly exact. You can ascertain the average ongoing value swings to make an objective. On the off chance that the average value swing has been 3 focuses in the course of the last a few value swings, this would be a reasonable objective.

When you've arrived at that objective, you can leave the exchange and appreciate the profit.

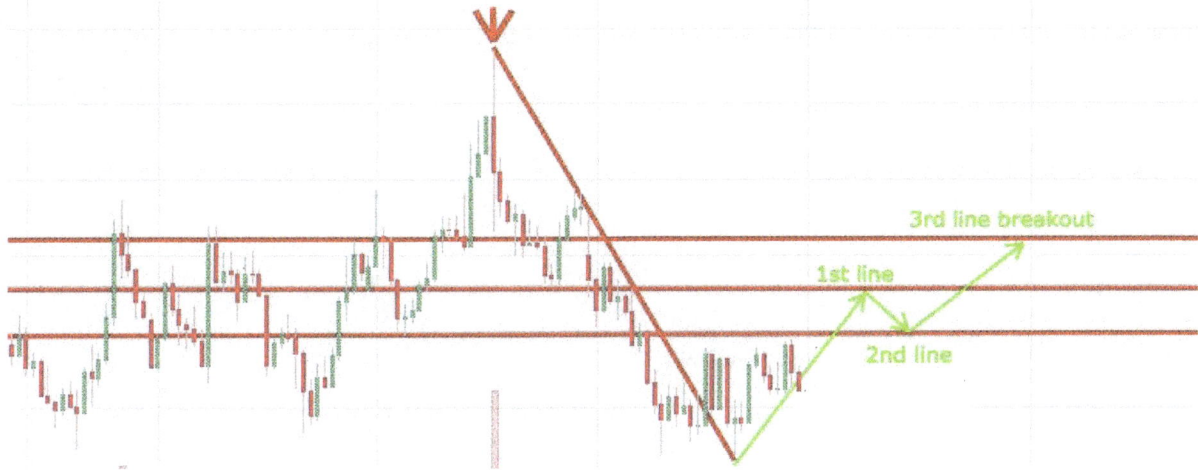

2. Scalping

One of the most well-known strategies is scalping. It's well-known in the forex market, and it hopes to gain by minute value changes. The main impetus is the amount. You will hope to sell when the exchange gets productive. This is a quick-paced and energizing approach to exchange. However, it tends to be dangerous. You need a high trading likelihood to try and out the okay versus reward proportion.

Be vigilant for unstable instruments, alluring liquidity, and be hot on timing. You can decide to wait for the market; you have to close losing exchanges as quickly as time permits.

3. Momentum

Well known among trading strategies for beginners, this strategy spins around following up on news sources and recognizing generous inclining moves with the help of high volume. There is consistently at any rate one stock that moves around 20-30% every day, so there's an adequate chance. You essentially clutch your situation until you see indications of inversion and afterward get out.

Then again, you can blur the value drop. Along these lines, around your value target is when volume begins to lessen.

This strategy is straightforward and compelling whenever utilized accurately. You should guarantee you're mindful of forthcoming news and income declarations. Only few moments on each trade will have a significant effect on your finish of day benefits.

4. Inversion

Albeit fervently discussed and possibly perilous when utilized by beginners, switch trading is utilized everywhere throughout the world. It's otherwise called pattern trading, pull back drifting, and a mean inversion strategy.

This strategy opposes essential rationale as you expect to exchange against the pattern. You should have the option to precisely distinguish potential pullbacks, in addition, to foresee their quality. To do this adequately, you need a top to bottom market information and experience.

The 'every day rotate' strategy is viewed as a special instance of turn around trading, as it fixates on purchasing and selling day by day low and high pullbacks/invert.

5. Utilizing Pivot Points

A day trading turn point strategy can be incredible for recognizing and following up on basic help and additional obstruction levels. It is especially valuable in the forex market. What's more, it very well may be utilized by run bound traders to distinguish purposes of passage, while pattern and breakout traders can utilize rotate focuses to find key levels that need to break for a transition to consider a breakout.

Figuring Pivot Points

A pivot point is known as a point of revolution. You utilize the costs of the earlier day's high and low, in addition to the end cost of security to figure the rotate point.

Note that on the off chance that you figure a turning point utilizing value data from a generally brief timeframe outline, precision is regularly decreased.

Anyway, how would you figure a turning point?

- Central Pivot Point (P) = (Low + High + Close)/3

You would then be able to compute backing and obstruction levels utilizing the rotate point. To do what you should utilize the following:

- First Resistance (R1) = (2*P) – Low

- First Support (S1) = (2*P) – High

The second degree of help and obstruction is then determined as follows:

- Second Resistance (R2) = P + (R1-S1)

- Second Support (S2) = P – (R1-S1)

Application

At the point when applied to the FX market, for instance, you will discover the trading range for the session regularly happens between the rotate point and the primary help and obstruction levels.

It's likewise important. This is one of the frameworks and strategies that can be applied to records as well. For instance, it can help structure a powerful S&P day trading strategy.

The breaking point Your Losses

This is especially significant in case you're utilizing edge—necessities for which are normally high for day traders. At the point when you exchange on edge, you are progressively powerless against sharp value developments. Indeed, this implies the potential for more noteworthy benefit, yet it likewise implies the chance of huge misfortunes. Luckily, you can utilize stop-misfortunes.

The stop-misfortune controls your hazard for you. In a short position, you can initiate a stop-misfortune over an ongoing high. For long positions, you can put it underneath an ongoing low. You can likewise make it dependant on volatility.

One mainstream strategy is to set up two stop-misfortunes. Initially, you put in a physical stop-misfortune request at a particular value level. Furthermore, you make a psychological stop-misfortune. Spot this at the point your entrance criteria are ruptured. So if the exchange makes an unexpected turn, you'll make a quick exit.

Risk Management

Stop-misfortune

Strategies that work consider. In the event that you don't oversee chance, you'll lose beyond what you can bear the cost of and be out of the game before you know it.

The cost may seem as though it's moving toward the path you trusted, yet it could turn around whenever. A stop-misfortune will control that chance. You'll leave the exchange and possibly acquire an insignificant misfortune if the benefit or security doesn't come through.

Insightful traders don't ordinarily hazard over 1% of their record balance on a solitary exchange. So in the event that you have £27,500 in your record, you can change up to £275 per exchange.

Position size

It will likewise empower you to choose the ideal position size. Position size is the number of offers taken on a solitary exchange. Take the contrast between your entrance and stop-misfortune costs. For instance, in the event that your entry point is £12 and your stop-misfortune is £11.80, at that point, your hazard is £0.20 per share.

Presently to make sense of what number of exchanges you can take on a solitary exchange, partition £275 by £0.20. That is the most extreme position you could take to adhere to your 1% hazard limit.

Additionally, check there is an adequate volume in the stock/advantage for ingesting the position size you use. What's more, remember that on the off chance that you take a position size too huge for the market, you could experience slippage on your entrance and stop-misfortune.

DAY TRADING TECHNIQUES

There are various day trading methods and strategies out there. However, all will depend on precise information, deliberately spread out in graphs and spreadsheets. Choices include:

- Swing trading

- Scalping

- Trading zones

- Trading on volume

- Arbitrage trading

- A basic day trading exit strategy

- Utilizing news

TECHNICAL ANALYSIS OF DAY TRADING

Technical Analysis: A Primer

The technical investigation is the investigation of past market information to conjecture the heading of future value developments. The system is viewed as a subset of security investigation nearby essential examination. Here we see how to utilize technical investigation in day trading.

It frequently diverges from the principal investigator, which can be applied both on a microeconomic and macroeconomic level. Miniaturized scale level major investigation incorporates the investigation of incomes, costs, profit, resources and liabilities, capital structure, and "delicate" components (nature of management group, serious position).

Large scale level basic investigation involves the examination or anticipating of financial development, swelling, credit cycles, loan cost patterns, capital streams between nations, work and asset usage and their cyclicality, segment patterns, national bank and political approaches and conduct, geopolitical issues, buyer and business patterns, and "delicate" information (e.g., notion or certainty studies).

A few traders may have some expertise in either, while some will utilize the two strategies to educate their trading and investing choices.

Most huge banks and financiers have groups that spend significant time in both principal and technical investigation. By and large, the greater the quality data one takes in to improve the chances of being correct, the better one's trading results are probably going to be.

FXTM is driving forex and CFD dealers. Offering an immense scope of markets, and 5 record types, they take into account all degree of trader.

Technical experts are frequently called chartists, which mirrors the utilization of graphs showing cost and volume information to distinguish patterns and examples to break down protections. Value examples can incorporate help, opposition, trendlines, candle designs (e.g., head and shoulders, inversions), moving averages, and technical indicators.

Presumptions in Technical Analysis

While a few traders and investors utilize both major and technical investigation, generally will in general fall into some camp or possibly depend on one unquestionably more intensely in settling on trading choices.

Technical experts depend on the procedure because of two fundamental convictions – (1) value history will, in general, be repetitive, and (2) costs, volume, and volatility will increase in general run in particular patterns.

We should experience each separately:

Market Cyclicality

Human instinct being what it is, with regularly shared conduct qualities, market history tends to rehash itself. The succession of occasions isn't able to rehash itself superbly, yet the examples are commonly comparable. These can appear as long haul or transient value conduct.

Business cycles are characteristically inclined to rehash themselves, as driven by credit blasts where obligation transcends salary for a period and in the long-run outcomes in money related torment when insufficient money is accessible to support these obligations. This will, in general outcome in moderate dynamic gains in stocks and other "hazard on" exchanges (e.g., convey trading) during an extension and a sharp fall upon a downturn.

Professionals verifiably accept that market members are slanted to rehash the conduct of the past due to its group, designed nature. On the off chance that conduct is for sure repeatable, this infers it tends to be perceived by taking a gander at past cost and volume information and used to foresee future value designs. On the off chance that traders can find openings where conduct is probably going to be rehashed, they can distinguish exchanges where the hazard/reward runs in support of them.

Along these lines, there is the inbuilt supposition in a technical investigation that a market's value limits all data impacting a specific market. While essential occasions sway budgetary markets, for example, news and monetary information, if this data is as of now or promptly reflected in resource costs upon discharge, the technical examination will rather concentrate on distinguishing value patterns and the degree to which market members esteem certain data.

For instance, in the event that US CPI swelling information arrives in a tenth of a rate higher than what was being evaluated into the market before the news discharge, we can pull out how touchy the market is to that data by observing how resource costs respond promptly following.

In the event that US stock prospects descend X%, the US dollar record builds Y%, and the 10-year US Treasury yield increment Z%, we can discover how such financial sources of info sway certain markets. Realizing these sensitivities can be important for stress testing purposes as a type of hazard management. For instance, if swelling were to out of the blue climb by 1%, we can utilize the information that focuses on respect to shock expansion readings to decide how the portfolio may be influenced.

Value, Volume, and Volatility Run in Distinct Trends

Another supposition behind technical examination (and all protections investigation all the more comprehensively) is that cost doesn't move as indicated by an "irregular walk," or as indicated by no noticeable or consistent example. Or maybe it moves as indicated by patterns that are both reasonable and unsurprising.

For instance, on the off chance that we take a gander at a graph of the EUR/USD from mid-2013 to mid-2017, we can perceive how technical examination assumed a job by taking a gander at help and obstruction inside the setting of the pattern. After the euro started devaluing against the US dollar because of a disparity in financial approach in mid-2014, technical experts may have taken short exchanges on a pullback to obstruction levels inside the setting of the downtrend (set apart with bolts in the picture beneath). After the pattern had blurred and the market went into a combination, a specialist may have decided to play the range and began taking aches at help while shutting any prior short positions.

Qualities

Initially, a technical investigation was a to a great extent a matter of "perusing the tape" or deciphering the progressive stream and greatness of cost and volume information through a stock ticker. As PCs turned out to be progressively boundless during the 1970s, information was incorporated into graph structure and turned into a professional's standard perspective.

Acknowledgment of graph examples and bar (or later candle) investigation were the most widely recognized types of examination, trailed by relapse examination, moving averages, and value relationships. Today, the number of technical indicators are considerably more various. Anybody with coding information pertinent to the product program can change cost or volume information into a specific indicator of intrigue.

Despite the fact that technical examination alone can't entirely or precisely foresee the future, it is helpful to recognize patterns, conduct proclivities, and potential jumbles in market interest where trading openings could emerge.

Expository Approaches

There are different ways to move toward a technical investigation. The easiest technique is through a fundamental candle value graph, which shows value history and the purchasing and selling elements of cost inside a predefined period.

(Week by week candle value graph of the S&P 500)

Others utilize a value outline alongside technical indicators or utilize particular types of technical examination, for example, Elliott wave hypothesis or music, to produce exchange thoughts. Some utilization parts of a few distinct strategies. Simultaneously, traders must oppose the possibility of "data over-burden" or jumbling graphs with such a large number of indicators and lines that it starts to unfavorably affect one's capacity to peruse the outline.

Traders may take an abstract judgment to their trading calls, staying away from the need to exchange dependent on prohibitive guidelines based methodology given the uniqueness of every circumstance.

Others may go into exchanges just when certain guidelines consistently apply to improve the objectivity of their trading and keep away from enthusiastic inclinations from affecting its adequacy.

Types of Charts

Candle

Candle graphs are the most widely recognized type of outlining in today's product. Green (or now and again white) is commonly used to portray bullish candles, where the current cost is higher than the opening cost. Red (or now and again dark) is normal for bearish candles, where current cost is underneath the opening cost.

It shows the separation among opening and shutting costs (the body of the light) and the all-out day by day go (from top of the wick to base of the wick).

(Candles appearing and down development in the S&P 500 list)

Open-High Low-Close

A candle outline is like an open-high-low-close diagram, otherwise called a bar graph. Rather than the body of the light demonstrating the contrast between the open and close value, these levels are spoken to by flat tick marks. The opening value tick focuses on one side (to show that it originated from the past) while the other value tick focuses on one side.

Line

A-line outline associates information focuses on utilizing a line, as a rule from the end cost of each timespan.

Region

A region diagram is basically equivalent to a line graph, with the region under it concealed. This is, for the most part, done to all the more effectively imagine the value development comparative with a line graph.

Heiken-Ashi

Heiken-Ashi outlines use candles as the plotting medium, yet take an alternate numerical definition of cost. Rather than the standard technique of candles deciphered from essential open-high-low-close criteria, costs are smoothed to all the more likely show inclining value activity as indicated by this equation:

- Open = (Open of past bar + Close of past bar)/2

- Close = (Open + High + Low + Close)/4

- High = Highest of High, Open, or Close

- Low = Lowest of Low, Open, or Close

Regular Terms

Average genuine range – The range over a specific timeframe, generally day by day.

Breakout – When value ruptures a territory of help or obstruction, regularly because of an imminent flood in purchasing or selling volume.

Cycle – Periods where value activity is required to follow a specific example.

Dead feline skip – When value decreases in a down market, there might be an uptick in cost where purchasers come in accepting the advantage is modest or selling exaggerated. Be that as it may, when venders power the market down further, the transitory purchasing spell comes to be known as a dead feline skip.

Dow hypothesis – Average. Advocates of the hypothesis express that once one of them drifts a specific way, the other is probably going to follow. Numerous traders track the transportation area given it can shed understanding into the strength of the economy. A high volume of product shipments and exchanges is characteristic that the economy is on sound balance.

Doji – A flame type portrayed by next to zero change between the open and close value, demonstrating hesitation in the market.

Elliott wave hypothesis – Elliott wave hypothesis recommends that markets go through repeating times of good faith and cynicism that can be anticipated and, in this way, ready for trading openings.

Fibonacci proportions – Numbers utilized as a manual to decide backing and opposition.

Sounds – Harmonic trading depends on the possibility that value designs rehash themselves, and defining moments in the market can be recognized through Fibonacci arrangements.

Momentum – The pace of progress of cost regarding time.

Value activity – The development of cost, as graphically spoke to through a diagram of a specific market.

Opposition – A value level where a prevalence of sell requests might be found, making value skip off the level descending. Adequate purchasing movement, for the most part from the expanded volume, is frequently important to rupture it.

Retracement – An inversion toward the overall pattern, expected to be impermanent, regularly to a degree of help or opposition.

Backing – A value level where higher greatness of purchase requests might be set, making value skip off the level upward. The level won't hold if there is adequate selling action exceeding the purchasing movement.

Pattern – Price development that perseveres one way for an extended timeframe.

Technical Analysis Indicators

Technical indicators include some factual or arithmetical change of cost or potentially volume information to give scientific portrayals of up/down development, backing and obstruction levels, momentum, pattern, deviations from a focal inclination, ratio(s), correlation(s), among different depictions. A few indicators additionally portray slant, for example, short intrigue, suggested volatility, put/call proportions, "dread" or "voracity, etc.

Technical indicators fall into a couple of fundamental classifications, including cost-based, volume-based, expansiveness, overlays, and nondiagram based.

Cost-based

Average Directional Index (ADX) – Measures pattern quality on an outright worth premise.

Average Directional Movement Rating (ADXR) – Measures the pace of progress in a pattern.

Item Channel Index (CCI) – Identifies new patterns or recurrent conditions.

Coppock Curve – Momentum indicator, at first expected to distinguish bottoms in stock files as a major aspect of a long haul trading approach.

MACD – Plots the connection between two separate moving averages, structured as a momentum-following indicator.

Momentum – The pace of progress in cost as for time.

Moving Average – A weighted average of costs to demonstrate the pattern over a progression of qualities.

Relative Strength Index (RSI) – Momentum oscillator institutionalized to a 0-100 scale intended to decide the pace of progress over a predetermined timeframe.

Stochastic Oscillator – Shows the present cost of the security or record comparative with the high and low costs from a client characterized run and used to decide overbought and oversold market conditions.

Trix – Combines to show pattern and momentum.

Volume-based

Money Flow Index – Measures the progression of money into and out of stock over a predetermined period.

Negative Volume Index – Designed to comprehend when the "shrewd money" is dynamic, under the supposition that the keen money is generally dynamic on low-volume days and not as dynamic on high-volume days. Indicator centers around the day by day level when the volume is down from the earlier day.

On-Balance Volume – Uses volume to foresee, resulting in changes in cost. Advocates of the indicator place belief into the possibility that if volume changes with a powerless response in the stock, the value move is probably going to follow.

Positive Volume Index – Typically utilized close by the negative volume file, the indicator is intended to show when institutional investors are generally dynamic under the reason they're well on the way to purchase or sell when the volume is low. Spotlights on days when the volume is up from the earlier day.

Williams Accumulation/Distribution – Looks at divergences between security (or record) cost and volume stream. This is intended to decide when traders are gathering (purchasing) or dispersing (selling). For instance, when value makes a new low, and the indicator neglects to likewise make an extraordinary failure, this may be taken as a sign that aggregation (purchasing) is happening.

Expansiveness

Expansiveness indicators decide how solid or shallow a market move is.

Advance-Decline Line – Measures what a number of stocks progressed (picked up in esteem) in a file versus the number of stocks that declined (lost worth). On the off chance that a file has picked up in esteem, however, just 30% of the stocks are up, yet 70% are down or nonpartisan, which means that the purchasing is likely just happening in specific parts as opposed to being certain toward the whole market.

In the event that 98% of the stocks are up yet just 2% are down or unbiased at the open of the market, it's a sign that the market may be increasingly trendless and "inversion to the signify" day trading strategies could be progressively powerful. Nonetheless, if a disproportionate development/decrease perseveres, it could imply that the market could be drifting.

Arms Index (otherwise known as TRIN) – Combines the number of stocks progressing or declining with their volume as per the recipe:

(# of propelling stocks/# of declining stocks)/(volume of propelling stocks/volume of declining stocks)

An incentive underneath 1 is viewed as bullish; an incentive over 1 is viewed as bearish. Volume is estimated in the number of offers exchanged and not the dollar sums, which is a focal defect in the indicator (favors lower cost per-share stocks, which can exchange higher volume). It is in any case despite everything showed on the floor of the New York Stock Exchange.

McClellan Oscillator – Takes a proportion of the stocks propelling short the stocks declining in a file and uses two separate weighted averages to land at the worth. Best utilized when cost and the oscillator are wandering. For instance, when the cost is making a new low; however, the oscillator is making another high. This could speak to a purchasing opportunity. Then again, when the cost is making another high, yet the oscillator is making an amazing failure, this could speak to a selling opportunity.

Overlays

Overlay indicators are put over the first value diagram.

Bollinger Bands – Uses a straightforward moving average and plots two lines two standard deviations above and underneath it to shape a range. Frequently utilized by traders utilizing a mean inversion strategy where cost moving above or underneath the groups is "extended" and conceivably expected to return inside the groups.

Channel – Two equal pattern lines set to imagine a combination example of a specific heading. A breakout above or beneath a channel might be deciphered as an indication of another pattern and a potential trading opportunity.

Fibonacci Lines – An apparatus for help and obstruction by and large made by plotting the indicator from the high and low of an ongoing pattern.

Ichimoku Cloud – Designed to be an "across the board" indicator that gives backing and opposition, momentum, pattern, and produces trading signals.

It was moving Average – A pattern line that changes dependent on new value inputs. For instance, a 50-day basic moving average would speak to the average cost of the previous 50 trading days. Exponential moving averages weight the line all the more intensely toward ongoing costs.

Illustrative SAR – Intended to discover transient inversion designs in the market. For the most part, suggested for drifting markets.

Rotate Points – Levels of help and obstruction decided from yesterday's open, high, low, and close. They were commonly utilized by day traders to discover potential inversion levels in the market.

Pattern line – A slanted line-shaped from at least two pinnacles or troughs on the value graph. A break above or underneath a pattern line may be characteristic of a breakout.

Non-Chart Based

Not all technical investigation depends on outlining or arithmetical changes in cost. Some technical investigators depend on conclusion based reviews from shoppers and organizations to check where cost may be going.

At the point when investor estimation is solid somehow, overviews may go about as a contrarian indicator. On the off chance that the market is amazingly bullish, this may be taken as a sign that nearly everybody is completely contributed, and barely any purchasers stay uninvolved to push costs up further. This may propose that costs are increasingly disposed to incline down. Or on the other hand, in any event, the hazard related to being a purchaser is higher than if the assessment was inclined the other way.

¥ WHAT STRATEGIES DO NOT FOLLOW IF YOU ARE EXPERT TRADER

¥ STRATEGIES THAT CAN BE FOLLOWED EVEN IF YOU ARE NOT EXPERIENCED

What is day trading? Day Trading is the straightforward demonstration of purchasing stocks with the goal of selling them at a greater expense (Short selling traders sell stocks with the aim of covering at a lower cost to make a benefit).

Unfortunately, most starting day traders will lose money. Trading includes a high measure of hazard and can make fledgling traders rapidly lose a huge number of dollars. Be that as it may, the appeal of day trading is the way that talented traders can make six figures working just 2-3 hours per day.

Most hopeful traders are looking for monetary opportunity and security and freedom. So as to be an effective trader, you should receive a trading strategy. My most loved is called Momentum Trading Strategy. That is what I'm offering to you here today.

Momentum Day Trading Strategy

Momentum is the thing that day trading is about. One of the primary things you ought to learn as an amateur trader is that the best way to benefit is by discovering stocks that are moving. Fortunately, pretty much each and every day, there is a stock that will move 20-30% or significantly more! This is a reality.

The inquiry is how we would discover those stocks before they make the large move.

Before going any further, how about we step back for a minute and ask ourselves what we require from a momentum day trading strategy. Above all else, we need a stock that is moving. Stocks that are slashing around sideways are futile.

So the initial step for a trader is to discover the stocks that are moving.
Trading Strategies for Beginners

Before you get impeded in an unpredictable universe of profoundly technical indicators, center around the nuts and bolts of a basic day trading strategy. Many tragically think you need a profoundly confounded strategy to succeed intraday, however regularly, the more clear, the more powerful.

The Basics

Consolidate the priceless components underneath into your strategy.

- Money management – Before you start, plunk down and choose the amount you're willing to change. Remember, best traders won't put over 2% of their capital at risk per exchange. You need to set yourself up for certain misfortunes on the off chance that you need to associate with when the successes begin coming in.

- Time management – Don't hope to make a fortune in the event that youjust allow an hour or two per day to trading. You have to continually screen the markets and be watchful for exchange openings.

- Start little – Whilst you're finding your feet, adhere to a limit of threestocks during a solitary day.

- Education – Understanding market complexities isn't sufficient; you additionally need to remain educated. Ensure you keep awake to date with market news and any occasions that will affect your benefit, for example, a move in the monetary arrangement. You can find a wealth of online cash related and business resources that will stay up with the latest.

• Consistency – It's harder than it would like to monitor emotions whenyou're five coffees, and you've been looking at the screen for an impressive timeframe. You need to let maths, methods of reasoning, and your system direct you, not nerves, fear, or avarice.

• Timing – The market will get unpredictable when it opens every day, andkeeping in mind that accomplished day traders might have the option to peruse the examples and benefit, you ought to stick around for your chance. So keep down for the first 15 minutes, you've despite everything stretched hours beyond.

• Demo Account – An absolute necessity has an instrument for any tenderfoot, yet additionally the best spot to backtest or explore different avenues regarding new, or refined, strategies for cutting edge traders. Many demo accounts are boundless, so not time confined.

Segments Every Strategy Needs

Regardless of whether you're after robotized day trading strategies, or learner and propelled strategies, you'll have to consider three fundamental segments; volatility, liquidity, and volume. In case you're to bring in money on little value developments, picking the correct stock is fundamental. These three components will assist you in settling on that choice.

• Liquidity – This empowers you to quickly enter and leave exchanges at anappealing and stable cost. Fluid ware strategies, for instance, will concentrate on gold, raw petroleum, and flammable gas.

- Volatility – This discloses to you your latent capacity benefit run. Themore noteworthy the volatility, the more prominent benefit or misfortune you may make. The cryptographic money market is one such model notable for high volatility.

- Volume – This estimation will reveal to you how frequently the stock/resource has been exchanged inside a set timeframe. For day traders, this is otherwise called 'average day by day trading volume.' High volume lets you know there's critical enthusiasm for the advantage or security. Expansion in volume is as often as possible an indicator a value bounce either up or down, is quick drawing nearer.

5 Day Trading Strategies

1. Breakout

Breakout strategies base on when the cost clears a predefined level on your outline, with expanded volume. The breakout trader goes into a long situation after the advantage or security breaks above the obstruction. On the other hand, you enter a short position once the stock breaks underneath help.

After an advantage or security exchanges past the predetermined cost obstruction, volatility typically increments, and costs will regularly incline toward the breakout.

You have to locate the correct instrument to exchange. While doing this, remember the advantage's help and opposition levels. The more habitually the cost has hit these focuses, the more approved and significant they become.

Passage Points

This part is decent and clear. Costs set to close or more obstruction levels require a bearish position. Costs set to close, and underneath a help, the level needs a bullish position.

Plan your ways out

Utilize the benefit's ongoing presentation to build up a sensible value target. Utilizing diagram examples will make this procedure considerably progressively exact. You can ascertain the average late value swings to make an objective. In the event that the average value swing has been 3 focuses on the course of the last a few value swings, this would be a reasonable objective. When you've arrived at that objective, you can leave the exchange and appreciate the benefit.

2. Scalping

One of the most famous strategies is scalping. It's especially famous in the forex market, and it hopes to gain by minute value changes. The main thrust is the amount. You will hope to sell when the exchange gets beneficial. This is a quick-paced and energizing approach to exchange, yet it very well may be hazardous. You need a high trading likelihood to try and out the generally safe versus reward proportion.

Be vigilant for unpredictable instruments, alluring liquidity, and be hot on timing. You can hardly wait for the market, and you have to close losing exchanges at the earliest opportunity.

3. Momentum

Well known among trading strategies for beginners, this strategy rotates around following up on news sources and recognizing significant slanting moves with the help of high volume. There is consistently at any rate one stock that moves around 20-30% every day, so there's an adequate chance. You just clutch your situation until you see indications of inversion and afterward get out.

On the other hand, you can blur the value drop. Along these lines, around your value target is when volume begins to decrease.

This strategy is straightforward and compelling whenever utilized accurately. Notwithstanding, you should guarantee you're mindful of up and coming news and income declarations. Only a couple of moments on each exchange will have a significant effect on your finish of day benefits. 4. Inversion

Albeit fervently discussed and conceivably hazardous when utilized by beginners, turn around trading is utilized everywhere throughout the world. It's otherwise called pattern trading, pull back inclining, and a mean inversion strategy.

This strategy challenges the fundamental rationale as you intend to exchange against the pattern. You should have the option to precisely recognize potential pullbacks, in addition, to anticipate their quality. To do this viably, you need inside and out market information and experience.

The 'day by day rotates' strategy is viewed as a one of a kind instance of turn around trading, as it focuses on purchasing and selling day by day low and high pullbacks/invert.

5. Utilizing Pivot Points

A day trading turn point strategy can be phenomenal for distinguishing and following up on basic help or potentially obstruction levels. It is especially valuable in the forex market. Likewise, it tends to be utilized by run bound traders to recognize purposes of the section, while pattern and breakout traders can utilize turn focuses on finding key levels that need to break for a transition to consider a breakout.

Figuring Pivot Points

A defining moment is portrayed as a point of rotate. You use the expenses of the prior day's high and low, notwithstanding the end cost of security to figuring the defining moment.

Note that if you learn a pivot point using esteem information from a for the most part short time allotment plot, precision is normally diminished.

Taking everything in account, how might you process a pivot point?

- The Central Pivot Point (P) = (Low + High + Close)/3

You would then have the option to discover sponsorship and restriction levels using the defining moment. To do that you ought to use the going with conditions:

- First Resistance (R1) = (2*P) – Low

- First Support (S1) = (2*P) – High

The second level of help and impediment is then decided as follows:

- Second Resistance (R2) = P + (R1-S1)

- Second Support (S2) = P – (R1-S1)

Application

Exactly when applied to the FX advertise, for example, you will find the exchanging range for the meeting every now and again occurs between the defining moment and the fundamental assistance and hindrance levels. This is because a high number of brokers play this range.

It's furthermore noteworthy. This is one of the systems and strategies that can be applied to records too. For example, it can help structure a fruitful S&P day exchanging methodology.

Purpose of imprisonment Your Losses

This is particularly noteworthy on the off chance that you're using edge. Necessities for which are regularly high for informal investors. Right when you trade nervous, you are continuously feeble against sharp worth advancements. Undoubtedly, this infers the potential for increasingly essential advantages. In any case, it in like manner suggests the opportunity of gigantic disasters. Fortunately, you can use stop-setbacks.

The stop-setback controls your danger for you. In a short position, you can put a stop-hardship over a progressing high. For long positions, you can put it underneath a continuous low. You can in like manner make it dependant on instability.

For example, a stock worth moves by £0.05 every moment, so you place a forestall incident £0.15 away from your passage demand, allowing it to swing (in a perfect world in the ordinary bearing).

One standard technique is to set up two stop-setbacks. At first, you present a physical stop-incident solicitation at a specific worth level. Besides, you make a mental stop-disaster. Detect this at the point your passage criteria are cracked. So if the trade makes a sudden turn, you'll make a speedy exit.

Forex Trading Strategies

Forex techniques are unsafe normally as you need to gather your advantages in a short space of time. You can apply any of the procedures above to the forex market, or you can see our forex page for point by point methodology models.

Digital currency Trading Strategies

Digital currency Trading Strategies

The energizing and unusual digital currency market offers a lot of chances for the turned-on day trader. You don't have to comprehend the mindboggling technical cosmetics of bitcoin or ethereum, nor do you have to hold a long haul see on their practicality. Basically, utilize direct strategies to benefit from this unstable market.

To discover digital currency explicit strategies, visit our cryptographic money page.

Stock Trading Strategies

Day trading strategies for stocks depend on a considerable lot of similar standards plot all through this page, and you can utilize a large number of the strategies delineated previously. Underneath, however, is a particular strategy you can apply to the securities exchange.

Moving Average Crossover

You will require 3 moving-average lines:

- One set at 20-periods – This is your quick-moving average

- One set at 60-periods – This is your moderate moving average.
- One set at 100-periods – This is your pattern indicator.

This is one of the moving-averages-strategies that produce a purchase signal when the quick-moving average traverses the moderate moving average. A sell signal is created essentially when the quick-moving average crosses beneath the moderate moving average.

In this way, You'll open a position when the moving average line crosses a single way, and you'll close the position when it crosses back the contrary way.

How might you set up there's very a pattern? You realize the pattern is on if the value bar remains above or beneath the 100-time frame line.

For more data on stock strategies, see our Stocks and offers page.

Spread Betting Strategies

Spread wagering permits you to estimate on countless worldwide markets without ever really owning the benefit. Besides, strategies are generally direct.

If you might want to see the absolute greatest day trading strategies uncovered, see our spread wagering page.

CFD Strategies

Building up a powerful day trading strategy can be entangled. In any case, pick an instrument, for example, a CFD, and your activity might be, to some degree, simpler.

CFDs are worried about the distinction between where an exchange is entered and exit. Ongoing years have seen their prominence flood. This is on the grounds that you can benefit when the fundamental resource moves comparable to the position taken, while never owning the basic resource.

For CFD explicit day trading tips and strategies, see our CFD page.

Local Differences

Various markets accompany various chances and obstacles to survival. Day trading strategies for a particular market may not be as successful when you apply them to Australia. For instance, a few nations might be doubting the news, so the market may not respond similarly as you'd anticipate that they should back home.

Guidelines are another factor to consider. Indian strategies might be customized to fit inside explicit principles, for example, high least value adjusts in edge accounts. Along these lines, get on the web and check cloud guidelines won't affect your strategy before you put your well-deserved money at risk.

You may likewise discover various nations have distinctive expense escape clauses to hop through. In case you're situated in the West yet need to apply your typical day trading strategies in the Philippines, you have to get your work done first.

What kind of duty will you need to pay? Will you need to pay it abroad and additionally locally? Minimal expense dissimilarities could have a huge effect on your finish of day benefits.

Risk Management

Stop-misfortune

Strategies that work consider. On the off chance that you don't oversee hazard, you'll lose beyond what you can bear the cost of and be out of the game before you know it. This is why you ought to consistently use a stopmisfortune.

The cost may seem as though it's moving toward the path you trusted; however, it could turn around whenever. A stop-misfortune will control that hazard. You'll leave the exchange and possibly bring about an insignificant misfortune if the advantage or security doesn't come through.

Astute traders don't generally hazard over 1% of their record balance on a solitary exchange. So in the event that you have £27,500 in your record, you can hazard up to £275 per exchange.

Position size

It will likewise empower you to choose the ideal position size. Position size is the number of offers taken on a solitary exchange. Take the distinction between your entrance and stop-misfortune costs. For instance, in the event that your entry point is £12 and your stop-misfortune is £11.80, at that point, your hazard is £0.20 per share.

Presently to make sense of what number of exchanges you can take on a solitary exchange, partition £275 by £0.20. That is the greatest position you could take to adhere to your 1% hazard limit.

Likewise, check there is an adequate volume in the stock/resource for ingesting the position size you use. What's more, remember that on the off chance that you take a position size too large for the market, you could experience slippage on your entrance and stop-misfortune.

Learning Methods

Recordings

Everybody learns in various manners. For instance, some will discover day trading strategies recordings generally helpful. This is the reason various representatives presently offer various kinds of day trading strategies in simple-to-follow preparing recordings. Head to their learning and assets area to perceive what's on offer.

Online journals

In case you're searching for the greatest day trading strategies that work, here and there online web journals are the spot to go. Regularly free, you can learn inside day strategies and more from experienced traders. What's more, web journals are regularly an extraordinary wellspring of motivation.

Discussions

A few people will gain the best from discussions. This is on the grounds that you can remark and pose inquiries. Additionally, you frequently discover day trading techniques so natural anybody can utilize it. Because of the restricted space, you regularly just get the fundamentals of day trading strategies. Along these lines, in the event that you are searching for additional top to bottom procedures, you might need to consider an elective learning apparatus.

PDFs

In the event that you need a point by point rundown of the greatest day trading strategies, PDFs are frequently an incredible spot to go. Their first advantage is that they are anything but difficult to follow. You can have them open as you attempt to adhere to the guidelines all alone candle graphs.

Another advantage is that they are so natural to discover. For instance, you can discover a day trading strategy utilizing value activity designs PDF download with a speedy google. They can likewise be quite certain. Thus, discovering explicit ware or forex PDFs is moderately direct.

What's more, you will discover they are equipped with traders of all experience levels. Thus you can discover for beginners PDFs and progressed PDFs. You can even discover explicit nation alternatives, for example, day trading tips and strategies for India PDFs.

Online Courses

Others will discover intuitive and organized courses an ideal approach to learn. Luckily, there is currently a scope of spots online that offer such administrations. You can discover seminars on day trading strategies for items, where you could be strolled through an unrefined petroleum strategy. Then again, you can discover day trading FTSE, hole, and supporting strategies.

Money Management

The truth is that a lot of traders, especially novices, started with a lot in their trading accounts and at the end of the day, they had little or nothing to boast about. Many of them lost their funds because of thoughtless actions or not following a well-crafted strategy. To manage your money well, there are some things that you have to do.

Choose The Right Lot Size Based On Your Capital

When you start at forex training or financial market trading, you will tend to learn about trading lots. What we mean by a lot is the tiniest trade size available that can be placed when you decide to trade currency pairs on the foreign exchange market.

Usually, brokers tend to talk about lots using increments of a thousand or a micro lot. You have to understand that the lot size determines directly, as well as shows that risk among that you are willing to take.

Using a risk management calculator or a top like that can help you know what the right lot size is, based on what your trading account assets are currently. This can be used either when you are trading live or you are merely practicing. It allows you to know what amount that can be risked.

Using Standard Lots

A standard lot has a hundred thousand units of the base currency in a trading account. If you have a base currency of dollars, this is a hundred thousand dollar lots. The normal pip size for a standard lot is ten dollars for every pip.

When the trade is against you by ten pip, this is a loss of hundred dollars. This type of lot is used by institutional-sized accounts.

What this translates to is that you should possess at least $25,000 to be able to carry out trades using standard lots.

A lot of forex traders tend to make use of either micro lots or mini lots.

To a novice, this may not seem glamorous, but when you keep the lot size proportional to the size of your account, your trading capital will be preserved, and you can easily trade with it for a long while.

Learn, Learn and Learn

The fact that it is quite easy to get involved in forex has led a lot of people to get involved without bothering to learn. To succeed in forex or any financial market for that matter, you need to learn. You should learn from live trading, experience, as well as reading up on forex literature. Don't forget the news. You spiel find out about economic and geopolitical factors that have effects on the preferred currencies of a trader.

The world of forex is ever changing meaning that you must keep yourself abreast with these changes in the regulations, market conditions, as well as global events.

While you undergo the research process, you should also consider creating a trading plan.

This plan should involve a method where you can screen and analyze investments, in a bid to determine how much risk should be expected when creating investment goals.

Use only a reputable broker

The truth is that the forex world isn't so regulated, unlike others, meaning that you may end up carrying out business with unscrupulous brokers. It is advisable that you only open an account with a National Futures Association (NFA) member if you want your deposits to be safe, and you are interested in the integrity of that broker. Use only brokers that are listed as futures commission merchant with the regulatory body of your country. If the broker isn't registered, avoid them.

It is also advisable that you study the account offerings of the brokers like commissions, leverage amounts, spreads, account withdrawal and funding policies and so on. You can find these out by talking to a customer service representative.

Utilize a practice account

Almost every trading platform out there has a practice account. This is also called a demo account or a simulated account.

The account permits traders to carry out hypothetical trades that do not need a funded account. Using a perceive account allows the trader to get used to order-entry techniques quickly.

Using a practice account allows the trader to learn, thereby avoiding a lot of mistakes in their trading account.

We had seen cases of when a novice trader erroneously adds to a losing position, when he intended to close the trade.

Several errors in the order entry could worsen to a big losing trade. Losing funds is not the only issue; you have to also battle with a stressful and annoying situation.

There is nothing wrong if you decide to try out order entries before you start to place the real money on live trading.

Keep Your Charts clean

When a forex trader creates an account, he or she may be tempted to use every tech assessment tool available in the trading platform.

A lot of these indicators are high in the foreign exchange market, but it is advisable that you reduce the hunger of analysis methods that you use to be efficient.

Making use of several similar kinds of indicators like three oscillators or as three volatility indicators may come off as being unnecessary. Sometimes, you may even get opposite signals. You should try and avoid this.

If you aren't using an analysis technique well, you should consider taking it out of your chart. It is also essential that you look at the total appearance of the workspace.

The hues, kinds and fonts of price hard such as candle bar, line, range bar, and so on that you use should craft out an easy-to-read-and-interpret chart, permitting you to respond to the ever-changing conditions in the market quickly.

Stop Loss Order Is Not Just For Preventing Losses

Stop loss orders are used a lot in preventing losses, but it does more than that. It can also be used in locking profits. If used for this, it is sometimes called a "trailing stop."

At this point, the stop-loss order is being set at a per cent height that is beneath what the current market price is, and different from the price that it was bought at.

The stop loss's price fluctuates the same way the price of the stock adjusts.

What this means is that if the price of a stock increases, you may have to battle with an unrealized gain. This means that you won't have the money with you until after the sales.

Making use of trailing stop permits you to allow your run, and still guarantee you an amount of realized capital gain.

It is important that you note that the stop-loss order will always be a market order, meaning that it would lie low, until the trigger price has been reached. This means that the price your stock may sell for may end up being a bit different from what you specified as your trigger price.

THE BEST INDICATORS FOR INEXPERIENCED TRADERS

The Popular Technical Indicators and How to Use Them to Increase Your Trading Profits

They are ever considered how to utilize technical indicators in trading? Well miracle no more, this book presents 7 mainstream indicators and the strategies you can use to benefit from their signs.

Technical trading includes evaluating diagrams and settling on choices dependent on examples and indicators.

These examples are specific shapes that candles structure on an outline, and can give you data about where the cost is probably going to go straight away.

Indicators are increases or overlays on the graph that give additional data through numerical figurings on cost and volume. They likewise disclose to you where the cost is probably going to go straight away.

There are 4 significant kinds of the indicator:

- Trend
- Momentum
- Volume
- Volatility

Pattern indicators reveal to you which bearing the market is moving in if there is a pattern by any means. They're now and then called oscillators since they will, in general, move among high and low qualities like a wave. Pattern indicators we'll talk about incorporate Parabolic SAR, portions of the Ichimoku Kinko Hyo, and Moving Average Convergence Divergence (MACD).

Momentum indicators disclose to you how solid the pattern is and can likewise let you know whether an inversion will happen. They can be helpful for choosing value tops and bottoms. Momentum indicators incorporate Relative Strength Index (RSI), Stochastic, Average Directional Index (ADX), and Ichimoku Kinko Hyo.

Volume indicators disclose to you how volume is changing after some time, what number of units of bitcoin are being purchased and sold over the long run. This is valuable since when the value changes, the volume gives a sign of how solid the move is. Bullish proceeds onward high volume are bound to be kept up than those on low volume.

We won't cover volume indicators here. However, this class remembers For Balance Volume, Chaikin Money Flow, and Klinger Volume Oscillator.

Volatility indicators reveal to you how much the cost is changing in a given period. Volatility is a significant piece of the market, and without it is extremely unlikely to bring in money! The cost needs to move for you to make a benefit, isn't that so?

The higher the volatility is, the quicker a cost is evolving. It reveals to you nothing about bearing, only the scope of costs.

Low volatility shows little value moves; high volatility demonstrates huge value moves. High volatility likewise proposes that there are value wasteful aspects in the market, and traders spell "wastefulness," P-R-O-F-I-T. So for what reason are indicators so significant? All things considered, they give you a thought of where the cost may go next in a given market. Toward the day's end, this is the thing that we need to know as traders. Where is the value going to go? So we can situate ourselves to exploit the move and bring in money!

As a trader, you must comprehend where the market may go and be set up for any outcome. You don't have to know precisely where the market will go, yet comprehend the various potential outcomes, and be situated for whichever one appears.

Keep in mind. Traders bring in money in bull AND bear markets. We exploit long AND short positions. Try not to get excessively appended to the heading of the market, as long as the cost is moving you can benefit. Indicators will assist you in doing this.

Right away, here are the superstars.

1) Bollinger Bands

Bollinger groups are a volatility indicator. They comprise of a basic moving average, and 2 lines plotted at 2 standard deviations on either side of the focal moving average line. The external lines make up the band.

Just when the band is tight, the market hushes up. At the point when the band is wide, the market is boisterous.

You can utilize Bollinger Bands to exchange both going and drifting markets.

In a going market, pay special mind to the Bollinger Bounce. The value will, in general, ricochet from one side of the band to the next, continually coming back to the moving average. You can think about this like relapse to the mean. The cost normally comes back to the average over the long haul.

Right now, groups go about as powerful help and opposition levels. On the off chance that the value hits the highest point of the band, at that point, submit a sell request with a stop misfortune simply over the band to secure against a breakout. The cost ought to return down towards the average and possibly to the baseband, where you could take benefits. Look at the screen capture underneath.

Bollinger Bounce, diagram by means of TradingView

At the point when the market is drifting, you can utilize the Bollinger Squeeze to time your exchange passage and catch breakouts at an opportune time. At the point when the groups draw nearer together (for example, they crush), it demonstrates that a breakout is going to occur. It doesn't disclose to you anything about course so be set up at the cost to go in any case.

On the off chance that the candles breakout beneath the baseband, the move will, for the most part, proceed in a downtrend.

In the event that the candles break out over the top band, the move will, for the most part, proceed in an upswing. Investigate the screen capture underneath.

Bollinger Squeeze and ensuing upwards breakout, outline through TradingView

In outline, pay special mind to the Bollinger Bounce in going markets. The cost will, in general, come back to the mean. In slanting markets, utilize the Bollinger Squeeze. It doesn't reveal to you what direction the cost will go, only that it will go.

2) Ichimoku Kinko Hyo (AKA Ichimoku Cloud)

Ichimoku Kinko Hyo (AKA Ichimoku Cloud) is an assortment of lines plotted on the graph. It's an indicator that estimates future value momentum and decides regions of future help and opposition. From the start, this seems as though an extremely intricate indicator, so here's a breakdown of what the various lines mean:

- Kijun Sen (blue line): Also known as standard line or gauge, this is determined by averaging the most elevated high and the least low for as far back as 26 periods

- Tenkan Sen (red line): The turning line. It's determined by averaging themost noteworthy high and the least low for as far back as nine periods.

  - Chikou Span (green line): Also called the loosen line. It's the present end cost plotted 26-periods behind.

- The Senkou Span (red/green band): The first Senkou-line is dictated byaveraging the Tenkan Sen and the Kijun Sen and plotted 26-periods ahead. The second Senkou line is dictated by averaging the most significant high and minimal low over the span of the last 52 periods and plotting it 26 periods ahead.

Ichimoku Kinko Hyo, outline by means of TradingView

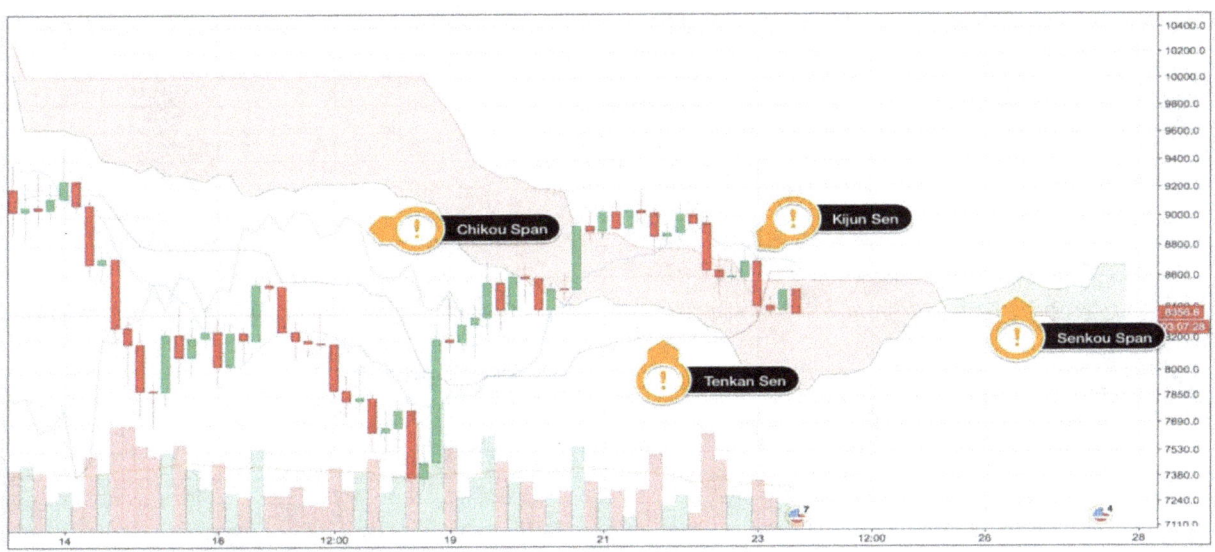

So how might you make an interpretation of these lines into trading benefits? I'm happy you inquired.

The Senkou range goes about as powerful help and opposition levels. In the event that the cost is over the Senkou length, the top line goes about as first help and the main concern as second help.

In the event that the costs underneath the Senkou range, the main concern goes about as the primary opposition and the top line as the subsequent obstruction. Basic as that!

Senkou range as powerful help and opposition, outline by means of TradingView

The Kijun Sen (blue line) can be utilized to affirm patterns. In the event that the value breakouts over the Kijun Sen, it's probably going to rise further. Alternately, in the event that the value dips under this line, at that point, it's probable it'll go lower.

Kijun Sen breakout into an upturn, graph through TradingView

The Tenkan Sen (red line) can likewise be utilized to affirm patterns. In the event that the line is going up or down, it demonstrates the market is slanting. What's more, on the off chance that it's moving sideways, at that point the market is running.

Level Tenkan Sen = running market, diagram through TradingView

Downwards Tenkan Sen = downtrend, graph by means of TradingView.

Keep in mind. The red line is a pattern indicator.

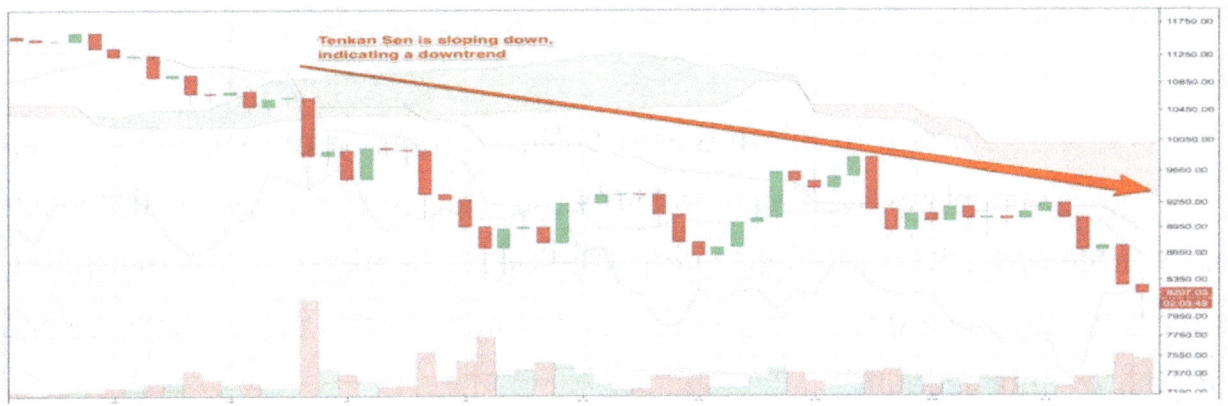

The Chikou length (green line) is plotted 26 periods BEHIND the present time frame. This is a key certainty to recall. It may be utilized as a pattern indicator of sorts. At the point when the line crosses the cost in a base-up course, the cost is probably going to go up. At the point when the line crosses the cost in a top-down course, the cost is probably going to go down.

Chikou Span crosses cost from top-down = beginning of a downtrend, graph by means of TradingView.

That is a ton going on in one indicator! What's more, a mess of data it can give you. You simply need to recollect what each line implies. In the event that you get your Kijun Sen and your Chikou Span stirred up, at that point, you could confuse a downtrend with an upswing. What's more, that'd be sad for your trading account!

3) Relative Strength Index (RSI)

The Relative-Strength-Index (RSI). This is a momentum-indicator plotted on a different scale. There's a solitary line scaled from 0 to 100 that distinguishes overbought and oversold conditions in the market. Readings more than 70 demonstrate an overbought market, and readings underneath 30 show an oversold market. Alright? Okay, we should perceive how you can bring in money from this person.

The entire thought behind RSI is to pick the tops and bottoms, to get into a market as the pattern is switching. This can assist you in taking a favorable position of the entire movie. Investigate the graph underneath.

Upturn after RSI shows oversold conditions, diagram by means of TradingView.

Around Feb 6, the market was profound into the oversold domain. This is a solid purchase signal. In the event that you had purchased the market here and hung on until RSI moved over 70 (around Feb 17), at that point, you would've gotten an incredible 490,000 pips! That is nearly $5,000 per BTC!

RSI can likewise be utilized to affirm pattern arrangements. On the off chance that RSI is over the 50 levels, the market is most likely in an upturn. Alternately, if the line is beneath 50, the market is likely in a downtrend.

In the model underneath, RSI showed oversold conditions on Feb 1–2. This resembled a decent purchase at that point. In any case, it turned out the be a fakeout. Perceive how it turned out…

RSI didn't leap forward 50 = fakeout, graph by means of TradingView

At first, the value began to rise, yet RSI didn't leap forward the 50 levels on Feb 4. What's more, you can perceive what occurred after that. The market dropped like a stone, right down to underneath $6,000.

In the past case of the upswing, you can see that RSI managed to achieve 50, despite the fact that it drifted around that zone for about seven days.

On the off chance that you're more hazard unwilling, at that point, sitting tight for pattern affirmation might be the best approach. It's an exchange off between 2 things. On the one hand, you remain to make more benefit by getting into a pattern early, yet you'll additionally not be right more frequently and conceivably lose heaps of pips to your stops.

Then again, you can trust that the pattern will be affirmed and be correct all the more regularly, yet you'll likewise miss a segment of the move so remain to make less benefit.

No one, but you can settle on that choice. I must give you the techniques and devices to play the game. However, you need to conclude how you're going to utilize them.

4) Moving Average Convergence Divergence (MACD)

Next on the list, we have Moving Average Convergence Divergence (AKA MACD). This is a pattern indicator, and it comprises of a quick line, slow line, and a histogram. Have you had an espresso yet? This will be a bit of befuddling, so focus!

The contributions for this indicator are a quicker moving average (MAquick), a slower moving average (MA-moderate), and a number characterizing the period for one more moving average (MA-period).

The MACD quick line is a moving of the moving average of the distinction between MA-quick and MA-moderate. Let that hit home.

The MACD moderate line is a moving average of the MACD quick line. The quantity of periods is characterized by MA-period.

At long last, the histogram shows the distinction between the MACD quick and moderate lines.

Try not to stress in the event that you don't get it the first time. We'll experience a model.

Let's assume you have MACD "12, 26, 9" (a typical default setting). This implies the quick line is the moving average of the contrast between the 12time frame and 26-period moving averages. The moderate line is a 9-period moving average of the MACD quick line. Furthermore, the histogram is the distinction between the MACD lines.

You may need to re-read that a couple of times to get it. What's more, ensure you do get it in light of the fact that MACD is an exceptionally valuable indicator.

So what's this "union disparity" thing about? All things considered, the moving averages and the histogram are plotted on a different diagram, and you'll see that the lines hybrid every once in a while.

MACD intermingling and uniqueness, diagram through TradingView

As the distinction between the 2 lines gets littler, they draw nearer together, for example, join. At the point when the distinction gets greater, they get further separated, for example, veer.

It's this attribute of the indicator that you can use in trading.

At the point when another pattern is framing, the MACD lines will merge, in the long run, they'll hybrid (demonstrating that the pattern has turned around), and the lines at that point begin to separate. At the purpose of hybrid, the histogram will vanish on the grounds that the distinction between the lines is 0.

Investigate the graph underneath.

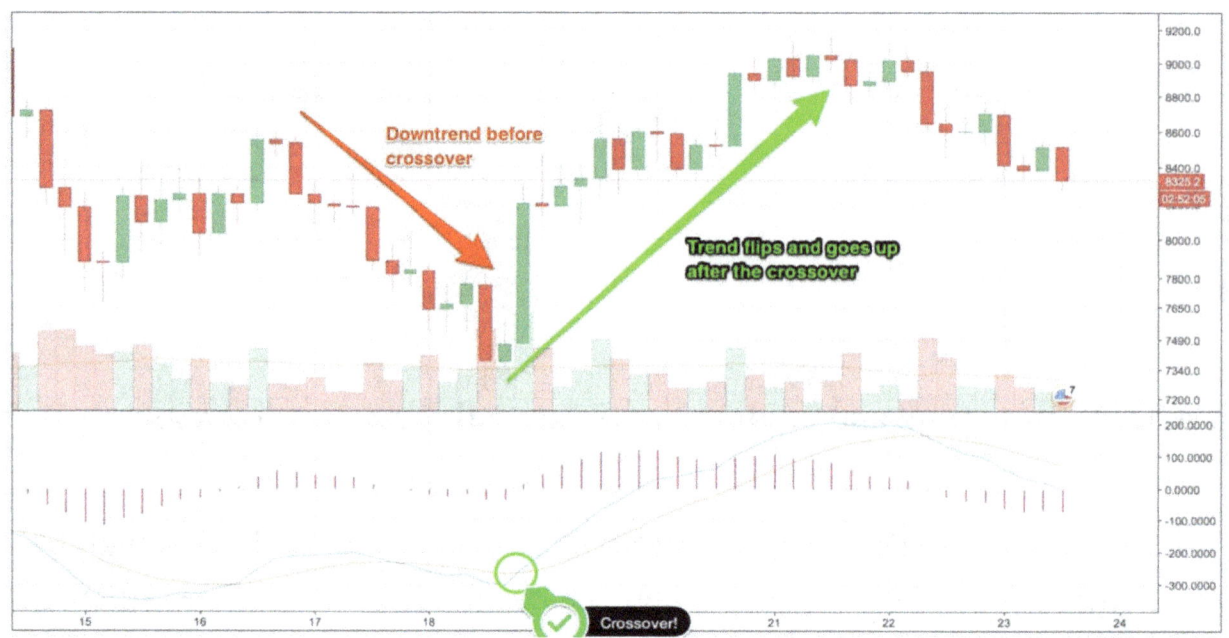

MACD hybrid, diagram by means of TradingView

The quick line (blue) traversed the moderate line (orange) around Feb 19. This shows the past downtrend has finished, and an upswing is beginning. Furthermore, would you see that… There's an upturn for the following hardly any days! Just about a 200,000 pip move and a decent $2K benefit for each BTC.

One important thing about MACD is that it's comprised of moving averages of other moving averages. This implies it lingers behind cost a considerable amount, so probably won't be the best indicator to utilize in the event that you need to get into patterns early. In any case, it's incredible for affirming patterns.

5) Parabolic Stop and Reverse (SAR)

Time to proceed onward to something somewhat less complex, Parabolic SAR. This is a pattern indicator. Specks are set on the graph above or underneath the cost, and they demonstrate the potential bearing of the value development. Does it get a lot easier?!

Illustrative SAR, graph by means of TradingView

In what manner can such a basic indicator be utilized in trading? All things considered, I'll let you know. At the point when the specks are over the value, the market is in a downtrend, showing that you ought to be short. At the point when the specks are underneath the value, the market is in an upswing, demonstrating that you ought to belong. Simple as pie.

Allegorical SAR focuses, graph by means of TradingView.

One thing to know about. Try not to utilize Parabolic SAR in a running market, when the cost is moving sideways. There'll be a great deal of commotion, and the dabs will flip from side-to-side, giving you no unmistakable sign.

Add Parabolic SAR to your trading arms stockpile and use it to understand solid patterns.

6) Stochastic

Next, the stochastic indicator. This is a momentum indicator and can be utilized to discover where a pattern may be finishing. Along these lines to RSI, it's utilized to decide when a benefit is overbought or oversold.

It's comprised of 2 lines plotted on a different diagram.

As you might've just speculated, stochastic can assist you with picking a passage point and get into a pattern at the absolute starting point. At the point when the stochastic lines are over 80, the market is overbought, and a DOWNTREND is probably going to follow.

Stochastic > 80 demonstrates the overbought market, graph through TradingView.

Presently when the stochastic lines are underneath 20, it demonstrates that the market is oversold, and an UPTREND is probably going to follow.

Stochastic < 20 demonstrates the oversold market, graph through TradingView

Indistinguishable provisos from RSI apply here. When attempting to get into patterns right on time, there will be numerous fakeouts, so you ought to be set up with stop misfortunes on the off chance that the market doesn't go your direction.

As usual, utilize the indicator to give you a thought of where the market is probably going to go. Try not to wager your home on it, however. Great hazard management wins.

7) Average Directional Index (ADX)

Here's another oscillator, yet this time it's a pattern indicator. Average Directional Index (ADX) values extend from 0 to 100 and are expected to invigorate you a sign of a pattern.

In the event that ADX is beneath 20, the pattern is powerless. On the off chance that it's over 50, the pattern is solid. Remember, however, that ADX doesn't reveal to you the heading of the pattern, only the quality.

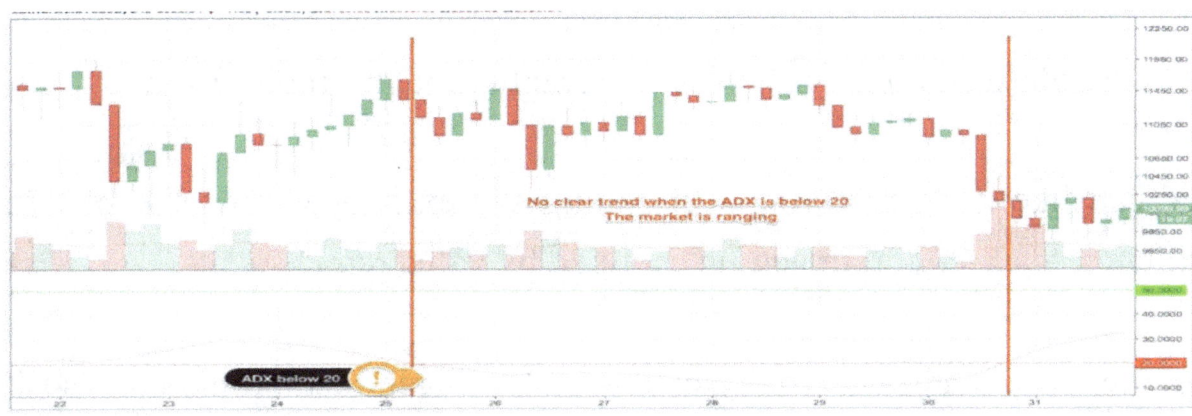

ADX underneath 20 (red line), the cost is extending, outline by means of TradingView

When trading, you can utilize ADX to keep away from fakeouts. It's truly best utilized in mix with different indicators, as (regardless of the name) it doesn't give you any data about pattern course.

Joined with a directional pattern indicator, for example, Parabolic SAR, ADX can affirm that a pattern is solid and is going to proceed. This should give you more certainty when going into a position.

ADX over 50 (green line), solid pattern, graph through TradingView

ADX can likewise assist you with exiting the exchange when the pattern debilitates, to abstain from getting captured by value retracements.

Likewise, with many pattern indicators, ADX lingers behind the cost, so it isn't valuable on the off chance that you need to get in on patterns early. Be that as it may, it is valuable on the off chance that you just need to exchange solid patterns.

Those are 7 famous indicators that you'll see around. Make your own outlines, mess with the indicators, and discover how they work.

Know, the default parameters for the indicators may be the best for digital forms of money, or for your trading style, so transform them. Perceive how the parameters influence the signs you get from the indicators, and whether this gives you better sections, or causes you to get better patterns.

Reward: Trading with numerous indicators

One major proviso to the entirety of the above mentioned. Trading from a solitary indicator won't make you rich. Every indicator has it's own confinements and won't be right 100% of the time.

Notwithstanding, you can utilize these indicators in the show to improve signs and, in general, make increasingly beneficial exchanges. Here are two or three guides to kick you off.

Illustrative SAR and Ichimoku Cloud

Trading with the Ichimoku Cloud and Parabolic SAR indicators, graph by means of TradingView

Here I've included the Parabolic SAR indicator and Ichimoku Cloud to a BTCUSD 1D graph. On day 1, the cost shut beneath the Kijun Sen (blue line), demonstrating that the cost may go lower. In the event that you were utilizing the Ichimoku without anyone else's input, you might've entered the exchange here. In any case, you're not, so hang on.

On day 2, there was a slight recuperation, yet the cost is still underneath the Kijun Sen, so still bearish. Allegorical SAR is still underneath the candle, a bullish sign. There's still clash between you're 2 indicators do as well, nothing. Endure it. Show restraint.

On day 3, there's a major drop in cost. We're presently path under the Kijun Sen, and look, Parabolic SAR has flipped sides, it's currently over the candle! The two indicators are demonstrating bearish signs, presently's an ideal opportunity to enter the market and go short!

You enter the market, and for the following 26 days, the market goes the manner in which you need. DOWN! In the event that you'd sold around $14K on day 3, you could've gotten more than 800,000 pips. That is $8K per BTC. A major success.

You can see that there were two or three fakeouts where the cost shut over the Kijun Sen (Jan 20 and 28). On the off chance that you'd just been taking a gander at the Ichimoku Cloud, perhaps you would've finished off your position. Explanatory SAR was as yet bearish, so it could've given you much-required data about where the cost was going.

RSI and Bollinger Bands

Here's another model where 2 indicators are superior to one. Utilizing RSI and Bollinger Bands, you can affirm when the market is turning and pick an extraordinary section point.

Toward the finish of October 2017, RSI began to show the market was overbought. This might've provoked you to sell! In any case, the Bollinger Bands were all the while extending, so no bones.

RSI kept on indicating overbought conditions through the start of November, and the market kept on ascending through this time. On the off chance that you'd repurchased in October, you would have genuine doubts at this point. The Bollinger groups have begun to contract, however, indicating that the market is getting tranquil.

Indicators are an extraordinary apparatus for you to utilize. They can assist measure with trading section, the course of the market, and in general, make you progressively certain to exchange. However, indicators don't excel without anyone else. They need a little assistance from their companions.

That is the reason consolidating indicators is an extraordinary method to give you more trust in your positions, maintain a strategic distance from fakeouts, and by and large get more cash-flow. It is anything but an impenetrable strategy. Nothing is, however, it will tilt the chances in support of you, and that is as well as can be expected trust in.

Evaluate your own mixes of indicators, see what works for you, what signals you can spot, and when you're agreeable to make exchanges. As I said previously, don't be hesitant to change the parameters and change the indicators; you may locate a brilliant blend.

By giving things a shot, you can characterize your own strategy. That is a definitive objective, to discover a method for trading that you can focus on and be certain that you're going to bring in money with.

WHAT STRATEGIES DO NOT FOLLOW IF YOU ARE EXPERT TRADER

An expert counselor can be portrayed as a definitive trading robot, which consistently screens markets and settles on an arrangement of trading choices for the trader. A genuine Forex EA will yield a great deal of money for the trader, while counterfeit EAs will plunge him/her into monetary ruin. There are numerous strategists who are building their unique EAs that perform uncommon trading stunts to yield results that may look great when they are really phony. There are different methods for spotting counterfeit expert consultants. This book will broadly take a gander at them.

Instructions to spot Expert Advisor tricks:

•   Check most extreme drawdown detailed in the backtest report of the mechanized trading framework;

•   Check if the part measures are expanding. There is a probability the strategists are utilizing martingale trading style to recuperate from misfortunes.

•   Check if the Forex robot utilizes the matrix style of trading, whereby thereis a great deal of purchasing and selling simultaneously. Such a strategy uncovered the record into a lot of risks and ought to be dodged.

• Check if Forex EA closes the exchanges merely seconds. Such tradingbots are utilizing scalping strategies and they, for the most part, don't deal with some other trading account since they are delicate to spread changes;

• Check if EA utilizes stop misfortune. Expert guides that don't utilize stopmisfortune can't shield traders from misfortunes and are in this manner not worth looking at.

• Check if exchanges are held open for quite a while. EAs that hold strategies for quite a while or those that nearby exchange seconds (scalping strategies) regularly produce incredible value bends, yet have no genuine pertinence in genuine trading.

Which sorts of Expert Advisors you ought to keep away from

In the first place, we should discuss the sorts of Expert Advisors and trading strategies that you ought to stay away from. Expert Advisors are significant with regards to robotized trading. Numerous individuals have been directed to budgetary ruin just on the grounds that an EA came up short on a little piece of detail. Everything about right now significant and ought to be taken into key thought.

Avoid strategies with very high drawdown figures.

Think about this backtests:

The outline speaks to a strategy report

For a great many people, this is a phenomenal trading strategy. Be that as it may, regardless of having an upward value bend and a 99% displaying quality (a great many people judge strategies by these two coincidentally), the outcomes are a long way from great. This is shown by the drawdown, which is at around 31% – a high add up to lose. Much more terrible, the relative drawdown is at 93%. In live trading, this strategy would not make due, as demonstrated by the relative drawdown.

Numerous traders are tricked by backtests basically on the grounds that they don't have the foggiest idea where or what numbers to take a gander at.

The value bend may trick apprentice traders or expert traders who have recently set out on an excursion to extreme trading utilizing expert counsels; however, for an expert, this backtest has not been progressed admirably.

Let us take a gander at the parcel sizes to appropriately clarify the imperfect idea of this backtest.

Avoid strategies with unthinkably large parcel sizes.

The exchanges start with 0.44 part sizes, and afterward, they keep on 8 parcels. When the strategy gets its first effective exchange, the part measures move again to an extremely modest number and afterward moves to parcel size 8. At that point, they hop to estimate 43. It is stunning that the parts continue expanding they go to 200, to 900, and afterward, they settle in thousands. No normal agent would permit his/her customers to exchange with 1000 parcel sizes.

For it to be even conceivable, the trading record ought to be incredibly large for it to have the option to execute such trading positions. More or less, these backtests glances great in its value bend, yet in all actuality, it is finished rubbish.

In this way, additional safety measures ought to be taken when managing strategies that twofold their parcel sizes. The motivation behind why swindlers utilize enormous parcel sizes is to endure the strategy tests and to make their strategies look great on the screen.
The graph speaks to the strategy with huge parcel sizes.

Avoid strategies that long open exchanges for madly extensive stretches.

Moreover, strategies that hold exchanges for significant stretches of time are bad. There are traders anyway who contend that they exchange for the since quite a while ago run, which is excellent.

Long haul exchanges stop to bode well when they keep going for quite a long while. They should keep going for half a month or months all things considered before they are shut.

From the model underneath, one trading strategy goes on for 1287 days, which is around three and a half years. Sensibly, who might ever hold a solitary exchange for over three years?

Precisely, no rational individual would show restraint enough to hold an exchange for a long time when there are such a large number of exchanges that could be made over a similar period.

It could be accepted that the proprietor of the strategy wouldn't like to lose any exchanges and needs to have the same number of wins as he/she can have, regardless of whether they are ludicrous.

There are other extraordinary exchanges that last between 300 to 900 days.

Before receiving such a strategy, you ought to ask yourself: why clutch a strategy that guarantees yearly returns when you can have the same number of exchanges as you need in the equivalent time period?

The figure outlines a strategy that holds exchanges for a significant stretch of time.

To additionally feature the issue of long haul exchanges let us take a gander at a trading report beneath:

The figure outlines a value bend with numerous drawdowns.

At the point when you appropriately take a gander at the value bend, you see that there are numerous drawdowns (pointed by the red bolts). The drawdowns speak to exchange places that have been held for an extensive stretch and afterward wound up in misfortunes. As much as the strategy picks up benefits, the quantity of drawdowns is high.

Besides, the reputation of the record isn't checked. This could imply that the strategy is created. Truly, OK, sit tight for that long and hold your losing position when you realize that they may wind up in misfortunes?

Avoid scalping strategies since they are touchy to Spread changes.

Shouldn't something be said about scalping strategies? Is it accurate to say that they aren't among the most mainstream expert counsels?

The facts demonstrate that they are famous as prove by the number of individuals who use them to scout for well-known markets. The issue with scalping strategies is that the greater part of them don't work.

You might be tricked by the attractive exchange results. However, like different strategies, they can be effortlessly created to deliver results that may tempt traders.

Moreover, scalping strategies are delicate to value changes. Along these lines, they, for the most part, don't chip away at most merchants.

On the off chance that a scalping strategy figures out how to chip away at one intermediary, at that point, there is a high probability that it will neglect to take a shot at another dealer. Truth be told, if the strategy was to be utilized again by a similar specialist, there is a high possibility that it will likewise fizzle.

Investigate the length of the exchanges the model given underneath:

The figure speaks to a scalping strategy

The length of most exchanges is zero seconds. The Pips are running in the hundreds in only zero seconds, and the average holding time is somewhere in the range of zero and three seconds. This is totally crazy. It is dubious that this strategy works in any genuine trading other than the demo account that it began from.

Avoid strategies with a massively enormous stop misfortune

Strategies with immense stop misfortune should likewise be maintained a strategic distance from except if you ensure your MetaTrader 4 record (MT4) with Equity Sentry Expert Advisor. Stop misfortune is fundamentally the capacity of a trading strategy to totally end trading positions when they begin making misfortunes. Along these lines, envision a strategy that doesn't utilize stop misfortune and the money related ruin that anticipates a trader that utilizations such a strategy.

A few people may contend that they don't utilize stop misfortune since they utilize shrouded stops. In the event that that is the situation, at that point, for what reason don't they utilize hard stops too?

Hard stops may be set to be two or multiple times greater than concealed stop misfortune, yet for a situation Internet association issue, you would not lose in excess of a hard stop misfortune. Along these lines, you have a higher possibility of controlling losing exchanges while utilizing shrouded stops and hand stops simultaneously.

For what reason would anybody consider utilizing strategies with no stop misfortune on the off chance that they posture such a substantial hazard to his/her benefits? There ought to be some degree of assurance at any rate against misfortunes, regardless of whether it is only half of it.

So if an EA doesn't offer hard stop arrangements like an assurance of the record's value, debilitating Autotrading, and shutting the exchanges, at that point, it ought to be disposed of.

Avoid framework trading Expert Advisors.

In conclusion, there are those strategies that utilization matrix trading style – this style includes making loads of purchasing and selling exchanges simultaneously with the point of making immense benefits. Making various purchase stops and sell stops simultaneously opens the record to high hazard and a bit nearer to catastrophe.

Stock Management

Building up Your Watch List

The first step when you are ready to get started in day trading is to do some research. When you first wake up in the morning, look over your notes and your research and then use that information to create a good watch list. This watch list can be important because it can limit you down to just a few options that you plan to use for trading on that day. There are thousands of stocks on the market and making this watch list will make it so much easier for you to pick the right stocks to invest in.

There are different methods you can use to create this watch list. But one of the best options is to use a scanner. These scanners can look for specific criteria that you want out of a stock and can make things faster than trying to look through them all on your own. To make the scanner work, you just need to list out the requirements that you want the stock to meet and then the scanner will alert you as soon as it finds one that meets these.

Decide Which of These Stocks Work Best for You

After the scanner has given you a few options for stocks that meet your requirements, you can decide which of these the best stocks are. You may have a specific strategy that you would like to go with and then choose the stock that seems to be following that strategy the best. You can always change strategies from one day to the next, or you can choose to stick with one strategy if it is serving your purpose.

As we discussed in some of our strategies before, make sure that you do not trade in the market for at least the first five minutes after the market opens. Some professionals wait even longer than these five minutes for the market to settle down.

There can be a ton of commotion and crazy ups and downs in the market during those first few minutes and investing at this time can hurt your profits. If you spend time looking at your scanner and then investigating the stocks that you receive, it will probably be at least five or more minutes before you are ready to enter the market anyway, but it is still important to be aware of this volatility and learn how to avoid it.

Put That Entry and Exit Strategy in Place

Now that you have a few stocks that are ready to go, you're probably excited to get into the market and start doing you is trading. Before you make that purchase, you need to finish up your strategies. This isn't just the overall strategy but also the center and the exit strategy so you know how to get into and out of the market at the right times.

The first strategy you should work with here is your entry strategy. This is the place where you are comfortable and will purchase your stock. Your aim is to get this entry point as low as you can so that you don't spend too much money and to increase your profits later on. When you look through the charts for that stock, you should be able to figure out a safe entry point that will provide you with a reasonable price on that stock.

Purchase the Stocks You Want

After you created your watch list and came up with your enter and exit strategies to keep you safe, it is time to actually go into the market and make your purchase. You will want to have all the criteria in place for that stock before doing this. But if you are working with a strategy, that is going to outline the criteria for you, so just follow that.

If you plan to work with your broker when doing day trading, you would just give them your order to get the trade started. The order is going to include a ton of information that can help the broker do everything that you want. This would include information on which stocks, in particular, you want to purchase, how many shares of each you want to purchase, how much you will spend on these stocks, when you want to enter the market, and when you want to exit the market. The broker is then able to take that information and place the order for you in the system.

There is also the option for you to do all of the work on your own. This is fine to do but most beginner traders are not going to pick this option because they worry about messing things up or doing something wrong. Make sure that if you are doing this choice that you work with a good platform that can get the work done quickly for you. If the platform ends up being really slow, or there are some mistakes done on your side, it could really ruin your trade.

Pay Attention to the Market Until the Trade Is Closed

You will quickly find that day trading has some differences compared to other stock trading options. Many other options are longer-term; you purchase the stock and then ride out the market, hoping that your choice will go up over some time. But with day trading, you are only letting the trade occur in one day. The purchase of the stock, as well as the sale of it, all need to happen sometime between open and close of the same day.

This does make day trading a riskier option to work with compared to some of the other stock trading options. This means that you need to really want the market and make some quick decisions on when to buy and sell your stocks. If you don't watch the market, then how are you going to be able to make these quick changes when needed?

Once you enter into a trade, you need to pay attention to the market and there may be times when the market changes quickly and you will need to make some quick changes to your position, or close it out, to help you earn more profits or keep the losses down as much as possible. Day trading is not one of those methods where you can place the order and then walk away. If you don't have the time to sit and closely watch the market, make sure to not place an order until you have more time.

Take Some Time to Reflect on That Trade and Write Down Some of the Information as Research Later

As a beginner in the day trading world, there are a lot of things to learn about the market. This is even truer if you have never invested in the past. As a trader, it is your job to learn as you go and make some changes if it is needed. But when you are learning a lot of strategies and keeping track of a large number of trades that are done in day trading, it can be hard to remember everything over time.

Getting a journal and writing down some of your mistakes, your tips, and more after each trade can make a difference. You don't have to write down a lot of information unless you want to. Just have a few lines or a paragraph. This may seem like it wastes your time. But if you ever get stuck on a trade later on, or if you are trying to figure out why you are in a slump and not getting the profits that you want, looking back through this information can make a big difference in how things go in the future.

Choosing and Purchasing Stocks

When buying a company's stock, a trader becomes a stakeholder or a partowner of that company. The value of the trader's investment, therefore, depends on the general well-being of the business.

Therefore, when buying a stock, a trader should start with a company that he or she knows. In so doing, a trader gets a place to start and avoids buying stocks without understanding how the company intends to make money.

Additionally, a trader should take into account the stock price and valuation. More experienced investors tend to look for securities that are cheap or undervalued to reap benefits when the stock price goes up.

Knowing How to Stop Loss

A broker places a stop-loss order once the stock reaches a particular level. A stop-loss helps to limit a trader's loss on a stock position.

For example, when a trader buys a share at $10 per share, he or she can place a stop-loss order for $8. Therefore, is the security's price falls beyond $8, the broker will sell the trader's shares at the prevailing market price.

A trader can know where to place his or her stop-losses by using the percentage method, the support method, or the moving average method. Many traders use the percentage method.

The percentage method involves calculating the percentage of stock a trader is willing to risk before he or she closes his or her position on the trade.

For instance, if a trader is willing to lose 10 percent of the value of security before he or she exits and the trader owns securities that are trading at $40 per share, the trader would place his or her stop-loss order at $36. That will be 10 percent below the market price of the security.

The support method also allows the trader to tailor his or her stop-loss level to the commodity that he or she is trading. As such, the trader needs to find the most recent level of support and place his or her stop-loss slightly below that level.

For example, if the trader owns a share that is currently trading at $30 per share, and he or she finds $25 as the most recent support level. Therefore, the trader should place his or her stop-loss slightly below $25. Placing the stop-loss slightly below the support level gives the commodity's price space to come down and bounce back up before the trader closes his or her position.

The moving average method requires the trader to apply a moving average to his or her security chart. A moving average is a technical indicator that analyzes the price changes of stocks while reducing the impact of random price fluctuations.

A trader may want to use a long-term moving average as compared to a short-term moving average to avoid placing his or her stop-loss too close to the stock price and getting closed out of his or her trade too soon.

As soon as the trader puts the moving average, he or she should set his or her stop-loss immediately below the level of the moving average. For instance, if the trader's share is currently trading at $30 and the moving average is at $26, he or she should place the stop-loss below $26, to allow the stock price space for movement.

Knowing When to Sell

A trader should start selling his or her stock when he or she miscalculated the decision to buy the stock, when the stock price shoots up dramatically, and when the stock has reached an unsustainable amount.

A trader will know whether he or she made a profit or loss the minute he or she sells the stock. While the buying price may help the trader to know how much advantage he or she has gained, the selling price guarantees the profit, if any.

While selling a stock should not be a common occurrence because trading in and out of positions could be detrimental to a trader's investment, postponing the decision to sell the stock when it is the right time to do so may also yield unfavorable outcomes.

For example, a trader may buy a stock at $20 to sell it at $25. The stock price reaches $25, and the trader decides to hold out for a couple of more points. The stock hits $27, and the trader still holds out to maximize on profit should the stock price move further up. Suddenly, the price drops back to $24. The trader waits until the price hits $25 again, but this does not happen. The trader then gives in to frustration and sells the stock at a loss when the stock price hits $18.

Consequently, if a trader sells at the opportune time, he or she will experience the benefits of buying the stock. However, the trader should not try to time the market because timely selling does not necessarily require accurate market timing. The focus should be on buying at one price and selling at a higher price, even when the higher price is not the absolute top.

When a trader discovers that he or she made an analytical error in buying a stock, the trader should sell the stock even if it means that he or she will make a loss.

If a trade does not meet the trader's short-term earnings predictions and the price of the shares takes a fall, he or she should not sell the stock if the business is not losing market shares to competitors. If the company loses market shares to competitors, then that may be a good reason for the trader to sell the stock.

Alternatively, a trader can sell his or her stock when the stock price rises dramatically in a short period for particular reasons. The trader should take his or her gains and move on.

Additionally, a trader could sell when the company's valuation is becoming higher than its competitors are, or when the company's price-to-earnings ratio goes beyond its average price-to-earnings within five or ten years.

However, when a company's earnings decline when the demand is low, and the company starts cutting costs. That would be a chance to exit the position before any further decline in the value of the company's stock.

In addition, a trader could sell his or her stock for financial needs. That may not be a good reason from an analytical point, but securities are assets, and traders have the freedom to cash in their assets when the need arises.

Conclusion

Thank for making it through to the end of this book. Successful day trading is a journey; it's not a destination. In this journey, you're going to change. In this journey, you're going to be challenged. Your level of discipline, self control, and your ability to look at the big picture over a long period of time are going to be tested. Accordingly, you need to look at the tools and tactics that I've mentioned in this book to help you get a proper context for day trading. Ultimately, it's your mindset that will determine if you'll be a successful day trader or not.

If you are new to the day trading business, this book will act as your guide. It will show you the map, the way of reaching your goal of becoming a successful trader. This book will tell you where to start, which steps to take in the journey of day trading, and finally, how to train yourself so that you can become a successful trader.

Please remember, you will not become a successful trader by just reading this book. You will have to practice the rope tricks this book shows you about day trading. When it comes to trading, our reaction to the market is more important than what happens in the markets.

Knowing is just half the battle. Action or applying what you learned is the other half of successful day trading. Without action, you have zero chances of becoming a successful day trader down the line. But if with it, you have a fighting chance.

You don't need to apply all that you've learned at once. Take baby steps, one at a time. The important thing is you start building momentum. The longer you put off action, the higher your risks are for failure.

Here's to your day trading success my friend! Good luck

CPSIA information can be obtained
at www.ICGtesting.com
Printed in the USA
LVHW060807050521
686548LV00013B/721